"A DESPERATE HOUSEWIFE'S SPIRITUAL JOURNEY"

REBECCA SEATON

WestBow
PRESS
A DIVISION OF THOMAS NELSON

WestBow Press books may be ordered through booksellers or by contacting:

WestBow Press
A Division of Thomas Nelson
1663 Liberty Drive
Bloomington, IN 47403
www.westbowpress.com
1 (866) 928-1240

ISBN: 978-1-4908-1665-4 (sc)
ISBN: 978-1-4908-1664-7 (e)

Library of Congress Control Number: 2013921379

Printed in the United States of America.

WestBow Press rev. date: 11/27/2013

CONTENTS

ACKNOWLEDGMENTS

A SPECIAL THANKS TO JESUS MY LORD, WHOSE FAITHFULNESS TO ME HAS ENABLED THIS BOOK TO BE WRITTEN. HIS CONSTANT ABIDING AND TEACHING HAVE COMPELLED ME TO SHARE WITH THE WORLD HIS GREAT LOVE AND FAITHFULNESS. ALL GLORY TO HIM WHO HAS INSPIRED ME TO KEEP ON KEEPING ON WHEN SO MANY TIMES I FELT LIKE GIVING UP!

TO MY DEAR HUSBAND, JACOB, FOR THE ENCOURAGEMENT YOU HAVE BEEN TO ME. I FEEL LIKE THE COUNTRY SONG "STAND BY YOUR MAN" SHOULD BE RENAMED ESPECIALLY IN YOUR HONOR, "STAND BY YOUR WIFE!" YOU HAVE BEEN SUCH A SUPPORTIVE AND VITAL PART OF MY SPIRITUAL GROWTH AS THE TWO OF US HAVE SERVED CHRIST AS ONE.

TO MY PRECIOUS SISTER, JO, ALONG WITH HER HUSBAND, BOB, WHO READ AND REREAD AND SPELL CHECKED THE MANY MISSPELLED WORDS OF MY INITIAL MANUSCRIPT.

TO MY WONDERFUL GODLY SON-IN-LAW, ISAAC SHAW, THE COMPUTER EXPERT, WHO SO FREELY GAVE OF YOUR TIME TO ORGANIZE THE CHAPTERS AND THE SECTIONS APPROPRIATELY. THANKS FOR YOUR EXPERTISE WORK. I AM SO GRATEFUL THAT GOD HAS BONDED YOU WITH OUR FAMILY.

TO MY FAITHFUL FRIEND, RITA HICKOX, WHO PROOFED AND EDITED THE MANY MISTAKES AND ENABLED THE MANUSCRIPT TO BE REFINED TO AN EXCELLENT READING POTENTIAL. BEFORE IT FELL INTO YOUR HANDS FOR EDITING, I WAS SURE THAT THERE WERE ABSOLUTELY NO MISTAKES IN MY WORK. HOW WRONG I WAS! THANK YOU RITA FOR YOUR MANY HOURS AND TENACIOUSNESS IN PERFECTING THE FINISHED PRODUCT!

AND LASTLY, TO THE READERS OF THIS BOOK. MY PRAYER FOR YOU IS THAT YOUR LIFE

WILL BE ENRICHED AND YOUR FAITH WILL BE STIRRED WITHIN YOU, AS YOU BELIEVE GOD FOR THE MIRACLES IN YOUR LIFE. HE WILL REASSURE YOU THAT HIS GRACE IS SUFFICIENT FOR YOU!

A DESPERATE HOUSEWIFE'S
SPIRITUAL JOURNEY

PREFACE

IN MY WILDEST DREAMS I NEVER EXPECTEDTHAT I WOULD BE WRITING A BOOK. SO MANY PEOPLE HAVE ENCOURAGED ME TO SHARE BY WAY OF BOOK THE GREAT THINGS GOD HAS BROUGHT ABOUT IN MY LIFE, SO HERE IT IS!

I HAVE SUCH A PASSION FOR WRITING AND HAVE HAD SEVERAL ARTICLES PUBLISHED IN CHRISTIAN MAGAZINES AND DEVOTIONAL BOOKS. OUR GOD IS AN AWESOME GOD! MY PRAYERS ARE THAT YOU WILL BE INSPIRED AND YOUR LIFE WILL BE ENRICHED BY THE MANY TESTIMONIES SHARED IN THIS BOOK. GET YOURSELF A CUP OF HOT TEA OR COFFEE, FIND A COMFORTABLE CHAIR, AND GET SET FOR ENCOURAGEMENT AND ADVENTUROUS READING: IF GOD CAN DO MIRACULOUS THINGS IN THE LIFE OF AN EVERYDAY

DESPARATE HOUSEWIFE, HE WILL CERTAINLY DO IT FOR YOU AS WELL! HE IS NO RESPECTOR OF PERSONS!

INTRODUCTION

TRIALS -WE ALL HAVE THEM. CAN YOU THINK OF ONE PERSON WHO LIVES COMPLETELY FREE OF THEM? EVEN JESUS HIMSELF ENDURED HIS TRIALS, BUT WITHOUT SIN. THE BIBLE TELLS US IN JAMES 1:2 TO CONSIDER IT ALL JOY WHENEVER WE ENCOUNTER TRIALS. I DON'T KNOW ABOUT YOU, BUT THUS FAR I HAVE NOT BEEN ABLE TO BECOME ENTHUSED ABOUT GOING THROUGH TRIALS AND TRIBULATION. I CAN NOT GET MYSELF TO COME TO THE POINT OF EXCITEDLY EXCLAIMING, "OH GREAT! HERE COMES ANOTHER TRIAL!"

I ONCE SENSED THE LORD EXPRESSING THAT IT IS NOT HOW WE GO INTO THE TRIAL; IT IS HOW WE COME OUT. AFTER ALL, AS THE THREE HEBREW CHILDREN SHADRAH, MESHACH AND ABED-NEGO, ENDURED AND CAME OUT VICTORIOUSLY, WE CAN DO THE

SAME. AS THE LORD WAS WITH THEM IN THAT FIERY FURNACE, HE HAS PROMISED TO BE WITH US AS WELL. AS WE PLACE OUR TRUST IN HIM, WE CAN COME OUT "SMELLING LIKE ROSES" RATHER THAN SMOKE. WE CAN BECOME BITTER OR BETTER AS WE GO THROUGH TRIBULATION. THE LETTER "I" IS WHAT CHANGES THE WORD AND IT IS I WHO MAKES THE DIFFERENCE BY NOT FULLY TRUSTING MY SAVIOR.

THOSE WHO READ A DESPERATE HOUSEWIFE'S SPIRITUAL JOURNEY WILL BE ENCOURAGED TO ENDURE THE TRIALS OF LIFE. THEY CAN IDENTIFY WITH THE EPISODES SHARED BY THE AUTHOR, AND DISCOVER THE FAITHFULNESS OF OUR GOD. IF GOD CAN DO IT FOR AN ORIDNARY HOUSEWIFE, HE CAN DO IT FOR ALL!

I
FOREWORD

CHAPTER ONE
THE BEGINNING

BEING BORN AS THE MIDDLE CHILD IN A CLAN OF FIVE CHILDREN MAKES A STATEMENT WITHIN ITSELF! MY MOTHER, WHO WAS A BORN AGAIN CHRISTIAN, WAS A STAY-AT-HOME MOM, AS WERE THE MAJORITY OF MOTHERS BACK IN THOSE DAYS. MY DAD, WHO COMPLETED ONLY A FOURTH GRADE EDUCATION, MADE A GOOD LIVING BY WORKING AWAY FROM HOME. HE WAS NOT A CHRISTIAN UNTIL AFTER THE DEATH OF MY MOTHER. HIS VIOLENT TEMPER CAUSED ME TO BE AFRAID OF HIM TO A DEGREE AND HAD A BEARING ON HOW I VIEWED GOD... NOT AS A LOVING HEAVENLY FATHER, BUT AS A HARD TASKMASTER.

I DID ACCEPT JESUS AS MY SAVIOR AT THE EARLY AGE OF TEN AT AN OLD FASHIONED TENT REVIVAL. MY YOUNG HEART ALWAYS STRIVED TO PLEASE MY SAVIOR. ALTHOUGH I TENACIOUSLY TRIED, I FINALLY CAME TO THE CONCLUSION THAT IT WAS IMPOSSIBLE TO BE "GOOD ENOUGH" TO EARN SALVATION. IT WAS A DIFFICULT, BUT NECESSARY LESSON I HAD TO LEARN IN LIFE. HOWEVER, IT WAS NOT UNTIL I BECAME AN ADULT THAT I QUIT STRIVING TO BE A "GOOD ENOUGH PERSON TO GET TO HEAVEN" AND LEARNED TOTALLY THAT SALVATION WAS A GIFT OF GOD.

I WONDER HOW MANY CHRISTIANS TODAY STRIVE TO BE ACCEPTED BY THEIR GOOD WORKS AND FAIL TO TRUST HIM FOR HIS WONDERFUL FREE GIFT.

"FOR BY GRACE YOU HAVE BEEN SAVED THROUGH FAITH; AND THAT NOT OF YOURSELVES, IT IS THE GIFT OF GOD; NOT AS A RESULT OF WORKS, THAT NO ONE SHOULD BOAST."

EPHESIANS 2:8-9 (NEW AMERICAN STANDARD)

CHAPTER TWO

LOVE AT FIRST SIGHT

AS A TEENAGER, I KEPT MYSELF PURE… A VERY DIFFICULT THING TO DO WHENEVER THERE ARE SO MANY TEMPTATIONS IN THAT BIG OLD WORLD! MY PURENESS WAS SUCCESSFULLY ACHIEVED, PARTIALLY BY MY DAD'S THREAT THAT IF I EVER DID ANYTHING I WAS ASHAMED OF, I WOULD NOT BE WELCOMED BACK TO HIS HOUSE TO LIVE WITH THE REST OF MY FAMILY. THAT CERTAINLY WOULD PUT THE FEAR OF GOD INTO A PERSON, AND ONE WOULD NEED TO THINK TWICE BEFORE GETTING CARRIED AWAY! I WONDER HOW DIFFERENT TODAY'S TEENS WOULD BE IF THEY HAD DADS WHO HAD BACKBONE ENOUGH TO MAKE A THREAT LIKE THAT. I WONDER IF THERE WOULD BE FEWER BABIES BORN OUT OF WEDLOCK.

DO YOU BELIEVE IN LOVE AT FIRST SIGHT? I TRULY BELIEVE IT HAPPENED TO ME. THE FIRST TIME I MET MY FUTURE HUSBAND, MY HEART BEGAN TO SKIP BEATS! MY OLDER BROTHER BROUGHT HIM TO A YOUTH MEETING AT CHURCH ONE PARTICULAR NIGHT AND HE ASKED WHO WAS THE GAL DRESSED IN YELLOW? AS MY HEART WAS POUNDING OUT OF MY CHEST, I QUESTIONED MY FRIENDS IF THEY KNEW WHO HE WAS. WHEN I DISCOVERED THAT HIS NAME WAS JACOB, WITH MINE BEING REBECCA, AND HIS NICKNAME JAY, AND I LIVED OFF OF JAY STREET, I JUST KNEW HE HAD TO BE MINE! WHAT A CONFIRMATION.

NINE MONTHS LATER, WE WERE MARRIED. WE ELOPED TO GATE CITY, VIRGINIA BECAUSE I WAS UNDERAGE. I ALWAYS TELL OTHERS THAT JAY WAS OLD ENOUGH TO KNOW BETTER!

MY HUSBAND AND I BOTH FINISHED COLLEGE AND MOVED TO HAMPTON, VIRGINIA, BEFORE BEGINNING A FAMILY. AFTER FIVE YEARS OF MARRIAGE, WE HAD A BEAUTIFUL

BABY GIRL, WHO HAS BEEN SUCH A BLESSING FROM HEAVEN FROM THE BEGINNING. FIVE YEARS LATER, WE FINISHED OUR FAMILY WITH A BOUNCING BABY BOY.

ALMOST FIFTY YEARS HAVE LAPSED, AND I AM STILL AMAZED HOW GOD PICKED THE TWO OF US FOR EACH OTHER AND JOINED US TOGETHER IN HOLY MATRIMONY. WE HAVE SEEN SOME ROCKY TIMES, BUT GOD HAS HELPED US THROUGH THEM ALL.

I SOMETIMES WONDER IF YOUNG PEOPLE WOULD TAKE THE TIME TO PRAY FOR THEIR FUTURE SPOUSES, WOULD THERE BE FEWER DIVORCES.

"THE LORD DIRECTS THE STEPS OF THE GODLY. HE DELIGHTS IN EVERY DETAIL OF THEIR LIVES. THOUGH THEY STUMBLE, THEY WILL NEVER FALL, FOR THE LORD WILL HOLD THEM BY THE HAND." PSALM 37:23-24 (NEW LIVING TRANSLATION)

CHAPTER THREE
DARKNESS SETS IN

AS A YOUNG MOTHER WITH OUR FIRST CHILD, I BECAME REALLY DEPRESSED. PERHAPS IT WAS THE BABY BLUES DEPRESSION, BUT WHATEVER IT WAS, THERE WAS A DARK CLOUD SETTLED IN OVER ME WHICH LASTED FOR YEARS. I REMEMBER RIDING IN THE CAR DOWN THE ROAD, LOOKING OUT THE WINDOW AND WOULD JUST BEGIN TO CRY FOR NO REASON. I WAS MEDICALLY CHECKED WITH NO APPARENT CAUSE FOUND FOR DEPRESSION. I REFUSED TO TAKE ANY MEDICATION ALTHOUGH AT TIMES I FELT LIKE SUICIDE WOULD BE THE ANSWER. I LOOKED FORWARD TO GOING TO BED AT NIGHT, BUT FOUND THAT SLEEP WOULD EVADE ME. IN THE MORNINGS I LOOKED FORWARD THAT THERE WOULD BE A RAY

OF HOPE FOR ME, BUT PEACE WOULD ELUDE ME. OH, HOW MISERABLE I WAS. I FELT AS IF I WERE DANGLING FROM A THIN STRING OF LIFE IN A DARK TUNNEL.

HOWEVER, THROUGHOUT THIS SEASON OF MY LIFE, I POURED MY HEART OUT TO GOD, CONSUMED HIS WORD, AND CONTINUED TO ATTEND CHURCH FAITHFULLY. MY HEART FELT SO COLD AND IT SEEMED AS IF GOD HAD ABANDONED ME. MANY DAYS, I WOULD WEEP WITH TEARS FLOWING DOWN ONTO THE PAGES OF MY BIBLE AS I READ. THIS WAS A TIME THAT I COULD TRULY IDENTIFY WITH DAVID IN THE PSALMS AND WITH JOB'S DIFFICULTIES AS WELL. I ALSO FOUND MUCH COMFORT IN THE BOOK OF ISAIAH. THIS WAS A TIME THAT I CONSUMED SO MUCH OF THE BIBLE; IT LITERALLY BECAME PART OF ME WITHOUT MY TRYING TO DO ANY MEMORIZATION. I HAVE FOUND THAT THOSE DAYS OF DESPERATION HAVE BEEN SUCH A VITAL PART OF MY MINISTERING TO OTHERS TODAY. HAD I NOT GONE THROUGH THIS DARK, DARK VALLEY, I WOULD NEVER HAVE FAMILIARIZED MYSELF WITH THE WORD.

THANK GOD THAT HE HAS GIVEN US HIS WORD TO COMFORT, GUIDE AND HEAL US. HE HAS ALSO ALLOWED US TO GO THROUGH DEEP VALLEYS AND BROUGHT US "OUT OF THE FURNACE" SO THAT WE MIGHT BE ABLE TO HELP OTHERS THROUGH THEIR DIFFICULT TIMES.

MY HEALING WAS A GRADUAL PROCESS OVER A LONG PERIOD OF TIME. I CANNOT PUT MY FINGER ON THE EXACT DATE OR EPOCH, BUT I CAN TESTIFY THAT JESUS IS THE GREAT PHYSICIAN, THE GREAT COUNSELLOR, AND THE GREAT "I AM!" I WAS ANOINTED WITH OIL AND PRAYED OVER MANY TIMES, BUT THE HEALING WAS NOT INSTANTANEOUS. THE LORD SPOKE THE WORD "EMANCIPATED" TO MY HEART ONE DAY. I WAS TOTALLY UNFAMILIAR WITH THAT WORD AND LITERALLY CHECKED OUT IT'S MEANING FROM A DICTIONARY. I FOUND IT'S MEANING TO BE "FREE FROM BONDAGE."

WAS THE LORD ACTUALLY TELLING ME THAT HE HAD LIBERATED ME FROM SATAN'S GRIP? YES! I BELIEVE SO, HOWEVER, I MUST ADMIT,

IT TOOK YEARS FOR ME TO LEARN TO WALK TOTALLY IN THAT EMANCIPATION.

I WISH TO ENCOURAGE YOU TO NEVER GIVE UP. IF YOU HAVE PRAYED FOR WHAT SEEMS LIKE ETERNITY AND YOUR PRAYERS HAVE NOT BEEN ANSWERED, JUST KEEP ON KNOCKING... THAT DOOR WILL EVENTUALLY BE OPENED IN GOD'S TIMING. GOD WANTS TOTAL HEALING FOR HIS CHILDREN. HE WANTS US TO LIVE THE ABUNDANT LIFE. HE IS ON OUR SIDE!

"DO NOT FEAR, FOR I HAVE REDEEMED YOU; I HAVE CALLED YOU BY NAME; YOU ARE MINE! WHEN YOU PASS THROUGH THE WATERS, I WILL BE WITH YOU; AND THROUGH THE RIVERS, THEY WILL NOT OVERFLOW YOU. WHEN YOU WALK THROUGH THE FIRE, YOU WILL NOT BE SCORCHED, NOR WILL THE FLAME BURN YOU. FOR I AM THE LORD YOUR GOD." ISAIAH 43:1-3 (NEW AMERICAN STANDARD BIBLE)

CHAPTER FOUR
MY FIRST HEALING

ABOUT THREE YEARS FOLLOWING THE BIRTH OF OUR DAUGHTER, WE SO DESIRED TO HAVE A SON. IT WAS TWO ADDITIONAL YEARS BEFORE WE WERE FINALLY ABLE TO CONCEIVE. A MISCARRIAGE MIDWAY BEFORE CONCEPTION CAUSED US TO BE VERY CAUTIOUS DURING MY THIRD PREGNACY. COMPLICATIONS SET IN AND I ALMOST LOST THIS BABY AS WELL.

SINCE OUR BABY WAS NOT DUE UNTIL MAY, WE DECIDED TO TRAVEL FROM VIRGINIA TO TENNESSEE TO VISIT MY PARENTS FOR CHRISTMAS. DURING OUR STAY I WAS SHARING WITH MY OLDER SISTER ABOUT THE WOES OF OUR DAUGHTER'S CONTINUOUS DOCTOR'S VISITS BECAUSE OF EAR INFECTIONS. MY SISTER URGED ME TO BELIEVE FOR HEALING.

SHE INFORMED ME THAT HEALING WAS INCLUDED IN THE ATONEMENT AND ALSO PART OF OUR INHERITANCE AS CHRISTIANS. I HAD NEVER REALLY ENTERTAINED THOSE THOUGHTS BEFORE.

THAT NIGHT, SOMEWHERE NEARING THE MIDNIGHT HOUR, I AWAKENED WITH A TERRIBLE SORE THROAT. I WAS SO UNCOMFORTABLE AS SLEEP EVADED ME; I BEGAN TOSSING AND TURNING. FINALLY I DECIDED TO GET UP AND RAID MY MOM'S MEDICINE CABINET FOR ANY TYPE OF SPRAY THAT MIGHT SOOTHE MY ACHNG THROAT WITHOUT THREATHENING MY UNBORN CHILD, BUT TO NO AVAIL. BACK TO BED I WENT, WITH THE CONTINUATION OF RESTLESSNESS. I FINALLY SETTLED DOWN LONG ENOUGH TO BEGIN THINKING ABOUT WHAT MY SISTER HAD SHARED WITH ME REGARDING THE SUBJECT OF HEALING. I REALLY DON'T THINK I HAD THAT MUCH FAITH ATTACHED, BUT WAS IN SUCH MISERY THAT I WAS WILLING TO TRY ANYTHING. I JUST MADE A STATEMENT WITHIN MY SPIRIT. I SAID, "LORD I KNOW THAT BY YOUR STRIPES

I AM HEALED." AND WITH EACH SWALLOW, MY THROAT WAS A LITTLE LESS SORE. BY THE THIRD TIME I SWALLOWED, MY THROAT WAS COMPLETELY HEALED! I WAS SO EXCITED, I FELT LIKE I NEEDED TO TELL SOMEONE, AND WHO BETTER THAN MY SISTER? TRYING HARD NOT TO AWAKEN ANYONE, I CREPT QUIETLY TO THE FRONT BEDROOM WHERE SHE AND HER HUSBAND WERE SLEEPING. TO MY AMAZEMENT, SHE HAD BEEN AWAKENED SUDDENLY WITH THE FEELING THAT SOMETHING SPIRITUALLY HAD JUST OCCURRED AND WAS SITTING UP IN BED. WHEN I SHARED WHAT HAD HAPPENED, SHE WAS NOT SURPRISED AT ALL, BUT I CERTAINLY WAS! I WAS AMAZED THAT GOD WAS NOT JUST A GOD WAY UP IN HEAVEN UNAWARE OF WHAT WAS GOING ON WITH A CHILD OF HIS. FURTHERMORE, HE LOVED ME ENOUGH TO TOUCH AND HEAL ME THAT NIGHT!

A SPARK OF FIRE WAS IGNITED WITHIN ME THAT NIGHT. I FOUND THAT EVERYTIME SOMEONE NEEDED A HEALING TOUCH, I WAS READY TO PRAY FOR THE NEED, WHETHER IN ONE OF MY CHILDREN, A FRIEND, OR EVEN

A STRANGER. SINCE THAT NIGHT, I HAVE WITNESSED MANY HEALINGS. I REALIZE THAT GOD IS ABLE TO HEAL SERIOUS DISEASES JUST AS EASILY AS SOMETHING AS SIMPLE AS A HEADACHE OR SORE THROAT.

SEVERAL YEARS LATER, I ATTENDED A CHRISTIAN CONFERENCE IN RICHMOND, VIRGINIA ON THE TOPIC OF HEALING. THE SPEAKER STATED THAT HEALING WAS JUST AS SIMPLE AS ASKING, THANKING THE LORD FOR HIS TOUCH OF HEALING AND THEN CONFESSING YOUR HEALING TO SOMEONE IN A POSITIVE MANNER.

I HAD SUFFERED WITH SERIOUS SINUS PROBLEMS SINCE TEENAGE YEARS. ORAL MEDICINE AS WELL AS ADMINISTERING PRESCRIPTION NASAL SPRAYS THROUGHOUT THE YEARS HAD BROUGHT SOME RELIEF. HOWEVER, I OFTEN FOUND IT NECESSARY TO SLEEP IN AN ALMOST- SITTING- UPRIGHT POSITION IN ORDER TO BREATHE PROPERLY.

I DECIDED THAT PARTICULAR NIGHT, AFTER HAVING HEARD THE TEACHING, I WOULD

TRY WHAT WAS SUGGESTED. I ASKED JESUS TO HEAL ME, I THANKED HIM AND AS SOON AS I GOT HOME, I CONFESSED IT TO MY HUSBAND, WHO HAD BEEN UNABLE TO ATTEND THE MEETING. I ALSO MARCHED TO THE MEDICINE CABINET AND THREW THE MEDS AND SPRAYS INTO THE TRASH! (I'M NOT SUGGESTING YOU TO DO THE SAME WITHOUT GOD'S LEADING.) I SLEPT LIKE A BABY THAT NIGHT AND SEEMINGLY HAD RECEIVED MY HEALING, AT LEAST FOR THE TIME BEING. ABOUT A MONTH LATER, ALL OF A SUDDEN, I BECAME AFFLICTED WITH THE SAME SYMPTOMS I HAD SUFFERED BEFORE. I WAS TEMPTED TO GO BACK TO THE DOCTOR FOR PRESCRIPTIONS, BUT I BEGAN TO REFLECT. I THOUGHT, "NOW LORD, YOU DIDN'T HEAL ME TO BRING THIS AILMENT BACK TO SURFACE. YOUR WORD STATES THAT YOUR GIFTS ARE WITHOUT REPENTANCE AND I KNOW YOU ARE TRUE TO YOUR WORD!" I THANKED HIM AGAIN AND REGAINED HEALING A SECOND TIME.

I HAVE OFTEN WONDERED IF SATAN DOESN'T ATTEMPT TO STEAL AND UNDO

WHAT THE LORD HAS DONE FOR US. I WISH TO ENCOURAGE YOU TO STAND UPON HIS PROMISES AND DON'T GIVE IN TO SYMPTOMS SATAN MAY TRY TO IMPOSE AFTER YOU ONCE RECEIVE YOUR HEALING.

"HE SENT HIS WORD AND HEALED THEM, AND DELIVERED THEM FROM THEIR DESTRUCTIONS." PSALM 107:20 KINGS JAMES VERSION

"BUT HE WAS WOUNDED FOR OUR TRANSGRESSIONS, HE WAS BRUISED FOR OUR INIQUITIES: THE CHASTISEMENT OF OUR PEACE WAS UPON HIM; AND WITH HIS STRIPES WE ARE HEALED." ISAIAH 53:5 (KING JAMES BIBLE)

CHAPTER FIVE

THE PIANO PURCHASED BY FAITH

A STRANGE HAPPENING OCCURRED WHEN OUR DAUGHTER, JACOBA (COBY), WAS ABOUT FIVE YEARS OF AGE. A VISITING LADY CAME INTO HER SUNDAY SCHOOL CLASS AND "PROPHESIED" OVER HER THAT SHE WOULD BE USED IN THE FIELD OF MUSIC FOR THE LORD. STRANGELY ENOUGH, COBY HAD DEVELOPED A TRUE DESIRE TO SING AND PLAY THE PIANO. THE ONLY PROBLEM WAS THAT WE HAD NO PIANO FOR HER TO PLAY! FOLLOWING IS AN ACCOUNT WHICH WAS MODIFIED AND PUBLISHED IN A CHRISTIAN MAGAZINE. ENJOY THIS WHIMSICAL VERSION I PENNED AS IF WRITTEN BY COBY HERSELF.

COBY'S STORY

MY LITTLE HEART FLIPPED SOMERSAULTS WITH SHEER EXCITEMENT AT MY MOM'S ANNOUNCEMENT ONE NIGHT DURING DINNER. HER SUGGESTION OF SAVING PENNIES, NICKELS AND DIMES TOWARD THE PURCHASE OF A PIANO ENABLED ME TO DEVOUR THE MUCH-DESPISED SPINACH FROM OFF MY PLATE WITHOUT BATTING AN EYE. USUALLY IT INVOLVED THE ENTIRE DINNER HOUR JUST COAXING ME TO TAKE A BITE OR TWO OF THAT DREADED STUFF. BUT THAT NIGHT WAS DIFFERENT.

AS FAR BACK AS MEMORIES CAN ALLOW, I LOVED TO SING. I BELIEVE I WAS SINGING LONG BEFORE I COULD EVEN SPEAK CLEARLY. POSSESSING A LOVE FOR MUSIC SO VERY EARLY IN LIFE, I WAS ALWAYS DRAWN TOWARDS A STRONG DESIRE TO PLAY THE PIANO AND TO SING. STRANGELY ENOUGH, AS IF TO CON-FIRM THIS FACT, A LADY WHO WAS TOTALLY UNFAMILIAR WITH ME, VISITED MY FIVE-YEAR-OLD'S SUNDAY SCHOOL CLASS ONE DAY, AND PREDICTED THAT I WOULD BE

USED IN THE FIELD OF MUSIC FOR THE LORD! THE VERY THOUGHT GREATLY PLEASED ME BECAUSE IT CONFIRMED MY HEART'S DESIRE.

MY UNDERSTANDING OF FINANCES SEEMED MUCH MORE ADVANCED THAN MY FIVE-YEAR-OLD BODY OR MIND INDICATED. I REALIZED THAT IT WOULD TAKE ALL WE COULD MUSTER TO EVER MAKE THIS SPECIAL PURCHASE OF A PIANO POSSIBLE.

OUR FAMILY, CONSTRAINED BY A STRICT BUDGET, EXPERIENCED LITTLE OF LIFE'S LUXURIES. I NOTICED AND ENVIED MY FRIENDS NEW CLOTHES AND TOYS WHEN MOST OF THE TIME, MINE WERE HAND-ME-DOWNS. I GUESS YOU COULD SAY WE DIDN'T HAVE MUCH, BUT WE SEEMED TO HAVE LOTS OF LOVE. MY MOM, WHO WORKED AT HOME AS AN OUTSIDE TYPIST, WAS WILLING TO CONTRIBUTE A BIG PART OF HER MEAGER EARNINGS TOWARDS THE PIANO FUND. AS I NOURISHED THE DEEP DESIRE TO FULFILL MY DREAM, I EAGERLY SACRIFICED EVEN MY BIRTHDAY AND CHRISTMAS MONEY TO THE FUND.

MOTHER SOMEHOW PULLED AN UNBELIEVABLE PURCHASE PRICE OF $400.00 OUT OF MID-AIR, AND SOON AFTERWARD WE BEGAN OUR LONG ROAD OF SEARCHING AND PRAYING FOR JUST THE RIGHT PIANO. WE DECIDED IT MUST BE A SLEEK CONSOLE WITH MODERN FEATURES - NO DILAPIDATED, OLD-FASHIONED INSTRUMENT WITH MISSING KEYS FOR ME. ONLY THE VERY BEST WOULD DO!

DAYS MELTED INTO WEEKS, THEN MONTHS. TWO YEARS SLIPPED BY AS QUICKLY AS SAND PASSING THROUGH AN HOUR GLASS AND I BECAME MORE AND MORE DISCOURAGED. IT SEEMED MY DREAM WOULD NEVER BE FULFILLED. DOUBTS BEGAN TO CLOUD MY MIND. I BEGAN TO WONDER IF GOD WAS EVEN INTERESTED IN A LITTLE GIRL'S PRAYER. AFTER ALL, TWO YEARS OF EARNESTLY PRAYING AND SEARCHING, WHICH SEEMED LIKE ETERNITY, WAS TO NO AVAIL. TO FIND A MODERN-LOOKING PIANO FOR THE PRICE WE COULD AFFORD SEEMED NEXT TO IMPOSSIBLE.

I FELT MY LITTLE HEART WOULD COMPLETELY BREAK, WHEN TIME AFTER TIME WE WERE TOLD THE PIANO WE WERE INQUIRING ABOUT HAD JUST BEEN SOLD. I REMEMBER ONE ESPECIALLY PAINFUL EPISODE. WE WERE VISITING MY AUNT IN ANOTHER STATE AND WERE SO EXCITED BECAUSE WE FELT WE HAD FINALLY FOUND IT! AS WE APPROACHED THE HOUSE OF THE PROSPECTIVE SELLER AND KNOCKED ON THE DOOR, I WAITED BREATHLESSLY WITH ANTICIPATION. WE INTRODUCED OURSELVES AND BARGED INTO THE HOUSE, WITH MONEY IN HAND, LOOKING AROUND ANXIOUSLY FOR "OUR" PIANO. WE WERE ABRUPTLY HALTED WITH THE BAD NEWS AND APOLOGIES THAT THE PIANO HAD BEEN SOLD ONLY MINUTES BEFORE. THE NEW BUYERS WOULD BE RETURNING SHORTLY TO TRANSPORT "THEIR" PIANO. THIS WAS MORE THAN I COULD BEAR. I WAS COMPLETELY DEVASTATED.

LATER, WHILE MOM WAS DRYING MY TEARS OVER ANOTHER LOSS OF AN EXPECIALLY CLOSE DEAL, SHE DECIDED IT WAS TIME TO STOP BEGGING THE LORD AND JUST BEGIN

BY FAITH TO THANK HIM FOR THE SPECIAL PIANO HE WAS PROVIDING FOR US. AS WE PRAYED AND OFFERED UP A SACRIFICE OF PRAISE THAT NIGHT, I COULD ALMOST ENVISION MY BEAUTIFUL PIANO. HOPE ONCE AGAIN BUBBLED WITHIN MY SPIRIT AS WATER SPRINGS UP IN AN ARTESIAN WELL.

ONE CRISP SPRING DAY A FEW WEEKS LATER, OUR FAMILY DECIDED TO GO FOR A BIKE RIDE AFTER DINNER. WE OFTEN ENJOYED THESE SPECIAL TIMES OF TOGETHERNESS ON SHORT EXCURSIONS IN THE NEIGHBORHOOD. THIS PARTICULAR DAY THE AIR SEEMED ESPECIALLY FRESH AND THE SKY A BRILLIANT BLUE. THE FLOWERS HAD NEVER SEEMED TO BE ARRAYED WITH SUCH VIBRANT COLOR AND BEAUTY. AS WE RODE ALONG, I WATCHED MOM AS SHE SUDDENLY STOPPED HER BIKE. SHE SWOOPED DOWN, RESEMBLING A VULTURE OVER ITS PREY, AND PICKED UP A NEWSPAPER LYING BY THE SIDE OF THE ROAD AND THREW IT AIMLESSLY INTO HER BASKET. OUR TIGHT BUDGET DID NOT ALLOW US THE LUXURY OF PURCHASING A NEWSPAPER, EXCEPT ON OCCASSIONAL WEEKENDS. AS SOON AS WE

RETURNED HOME, FROM FORCE OF HABIT, SHE BEGAN SCANNING THE CLASSIFIED ADS. SHE LATER TOLD ME IT WAS AS IF SOMEONE HAD WHISPERED IN HER EAR THAT THERE WAS NO USE TO EVEN LOOK-- WE HAD BEEN UNSUCCESSFUL UP TO NOW AND PROBABLY WOULD NEVER FIND THAT SPECIAL PIANO. AFTER ALL, THAT HAPPENED TO BE A MORNING EDITION OF THE WEDNESDAY PAPER. HAD THERE BEEN A PIANO FOR SALE, IT WOULD ALREADY HAVE BEEN SOLD BY NOW. NONETHELESS, MOM, BEING A VERY PERSISTENT AND STUBBORN LADY AT TIMES, DECIDED TO TAKE A LOOK ANYWAY.

TO OUR UTTER AMAZEMENT, A RELATIVELY NEW PIANO WAS ADVERTISED FOR THE REMARKABLE PRICE OF $400.00. UPON INQUIRING, WE FOUND THAT IT HAD BEEN ADVERTISED SINCE THE PREVIOUS SATURDAY, BUT NO ONE HAD EVEN CALLED TO ASK ABOUT IT. MIRACLE OF MIRACLES? YOU SEE, WHAT WAS EVEN MORE AMAZING WAS THAT THE OWNER OF THE PIANO WAS A RETIRED MINISTER OF OUR SAME DENOMINATIONAL BACKGROUND IN A NEARBY CITY. HE HAD

BEEN PRAYING FOR JUST THE RIGHT BUYER. I BELIEVE GOD HONORED OUR PRAYERS AND SAVED THAT SPECIAL PURCHASE JUST FOR ME. MY HEART SANG WITH JOY ALL THE WAY ENROUTE TO PICK UP MY NEW INSTRUMENT. THAT WEDNESDAY NIGHT WE WERE A LITTLE LATE ARRIVING FOR CHURCH. THE SERVICE THAT EVENING INCLUDED A TIME OF TESTIMONIES -- UP-TO-DATE ACCOUNTS OF WHAT GOD HAD BEEN DOING FOR DIFFERENT MEMBERS OF THE CONGREGATION. DID WE HAVE A PRAISE REPORT HOT OFF THE GRIDDLE FOR THAT SERVICE!

THE YEARS HAVE SINCE COME AND GONE. EACH TIME I SIT DOWN TO LOSE MYSELF IN MUSIC AND MY FINGERS FLOW SPONTANEOUSLY OVER THOSE OLD FAMILIAR KEYS, I CAN'T HELP BUT REMINISCE. I RECALL HOW FAITHFUL GOD WAS TO ANSWER A LITTLE GIRL'S PRAYERS IN HIS OWN TIMING, AND ONCE AGAIN, MY FAITH IS STRENGTHENED. I EARNESTLY BELIEVE THIS WAS A LESSON OF FAITH THAT BOTH MOM AND I SHALL ALWAYS REMEMBER.

AN UPDATED NOTE- COBY STILL USES THAT PIANO PURCHASED BY FAITH TODAY IN HER HOME TO TEACH TWENTY PLUS STUDENTS MUSIC LESSONS!

"DELIGHT YOURSELF IN THE LORD; AND HE WILL GIVE YOU THE DESIRES OF YOUR HEART." PSALM 37:4 (NEW AMERICAN STANDARD BIBLE)

CHAPTER SIX

IS THAT YOU SPEAKING, LORD??

HAVE YOU EVER WONDERED HOW GOD SPEAKS TO US LITTLE OLE HUMAN BEINGS? I HAVE IN THE PAST, BUT HAVE SINCE LEARNED HOW TO LISTEN FOR HIS STILL, SMALL VOICE. I AM AWARE THAT HE SPEAKS THROUGH HIS WORD, THE BIBLE, THROUGH PASTORS' MESSAGES AND JUST THROUGH INDIVIDUAL CIRCUMSTANCES. HOWEVER, YEARS AGO, I LEARNED HE SPOKE THROUGH OTHER MEANS AS WELL.

WHEN MY CHILDREN WERE PRESCHOOLERS, I OCCASSIONALLY TOOK THEM TO THE LOCAL NEIGHBORHOOD LIBRARY FOR A WEEKLY CHILDREN'S FILM/MOVIE. IT WAS ALWAYS

SOMETHING THEY LOOKED FORWARD TO AND TO BE PERFECTLY HONEST, I DID AS WELL. IT WAS AN OPPORTUNITY FOR ME TO KICK OFF MY SHOES, RELAX AND THUMB THROUGH A MAGAZINE WHILE THEY WERE SAFELY BEING ENTERTAINED.

ONE PARTICULAR DAY AS I WAS STRAIGHTENING THE HOUSE BEFORE LEAVING FOR OUR LIBRARY OUTING, THE THOUGHT CAME TO ME TO CALL A FRIEND, LINDA, AND INVITE HER TO JOIN US. HER CHILDREN WOULD ALSO ENJOY WATCHING THE MOVIE. I WAS NOT ESPECIALLY EXCITED ABOUT THE THOUGHT, SINCE SHE WAS NOT A REAL CLOSE FRIEND, SO I DISMISSED IT FROM MY MIND. BESIDES THERE WAS NO SIGNIFICANT SPIRITUALITY ABOUT THE NOTION, RIGHT? HOWEVER, THE THOUGHT WAS PERSISTANT AND IT COULD NOT BE DISMISSED THAT EASILY. FINALLY, I WAS AGGRAVATED ENOUGH TO CALL AND INVITE HER, IN ORDEER TO PUT THAT PERSISTANT THOUGHT TO AN END. TO MY SURPRISE, SHE CORDIALLY ACCEPTED MY INVITATION.

AT THE LIBRARY WHILE THE CHILDREN WERE ENGROSSED IN THE KID'S MOVIE, LINDA SHARED WITH ME THAT SHE HAD RECENTLY BEEN DOWN AND OUT. AS A MATTER OF FACT, SHE HAD GOTTEN SO DEPRESSED, THAT SHE HAD CRIED OUT TO GOD FOR HELP. SHE HAD ASKED HIM TO HAVE SOMEONE CALL TO CHEER HER UP AND ENCOURAGE HER. SHE HAD EVEN MENTIONED MY NAME TO HIM, JUST MINUTES BEFORE HER PHONE RANG! COINCIDENCE?

I THINK NOT. I HAVE COME TO BELIEVE THAT THESE PERSISTENT THOUGHTS ARE THE STILL, SMALL VOICE OF GOD ATTEMPTING TO GET OUR ATTENTION. I HAVE LEARNED TO LISTEN AND THEN OBEY. IF IT IS SOMETHING VERY DIFFICULT I AM ASKED TO DO, I FREQUENTLY ASK FOR A CONFIRMATION AND USUALLY HE DOES CONFIRM. JUST BE STILL AND KNOW THAT HE IS GOD.

"BUT THE LORD WAS NOT IN THE FIRE: AND AFTER THE FIRE A STILL SMALL VOICE."

I KINGS 19:12 (KING JAMES VERSION)

CHAPTER SEVEN

ROCKY MARRIAGE MIRACLE

IT HAS BEEN SAID THAT A LOT OF MARRIAGES HIT A SNAG IN STORMY WATERS BETWEEN THE SEVENTH AND TENTH YEARS. OURS WAS NO EXCEPTION. SOMETIME DURING THE EIGHTH YEAR, WE HAD BECOME LIKE TWO STRANGERS LIVING UNDER THE SAME ROOF NOT COMMUNICATING, EXCEPT DURING TIMES OF INTIMACY. WE WERE TAKING EACH OTHER FOR GRANTED AND THE ENTIRE SPARK OF LOVE HAD DISSOLVED. AS A MATTER OF FACT, I HAD LOST ALL AFFECTION FOR MY HUSBAND, WHOM I HAD BEEN SO MADLY IN LOVE WITH IN THE BEGINNING OF OUR MARRIAGE.

MY HUSBAND WAS THE BABY OF FOUR SIBLINGS AND QUITE FRANKLY, HE HAD BEEN SPOILED

ROTTEN. HE WAS VERY SELF CENTERED AND WAS DIFFICULT TO LIVE WITH. SINCE THERE WERE NO GROUNDS FOR DIVORCE, I BEGAN PRAYING ABOUT THE SITUATION. GOD SEEMED TO INSTRUCT ME TO PRAY FOR HIM AS MY ENEMY IF I COULDN'T PRAY FOR HIM AS MY HUSBAND OR AS EVEN MY CHRISTIAN BROTHER.

ONE NIGHT I DIDN'T THINK I COULD TAKE THE TURMOIL ANY LONGER AND I WANTED TO LEAVE HIM. AT THE TIME, WE HAD OUR THREE- YEAR- OLD DAUGHTER AND I HAD NO IDEA WHERE TO GO. THAT NIGHT AS I POURED OUT MY DISTRAUGHT HEART, WE BEGAN TO TALK. HE INFORMED ME THAT I WAS NOT "MISS PERFECT WIFE". HE LET ME KNOW THAT I HAD HURT HIM AS WELL, UNINTENTIONALLY, BUT NONE THE LESS, IT HAD HAPPENED. HE FELT THAT I HAD EMBARRASSED HIM IN PUBLIC MANY TIMES BY TELLING THINGS I THOUGHT HUMOROUS OF HIM, BUT HE DID NOT TAKE IT AS FUN. HE HAD BOTTLED THESE THINGS IN HIS HEART OVER THE YEARS. HE HAD NOT COMMUNICATED THE HURT I WAS CAUSING HIM.

WE STAYED AWAKE THAT PARTICULAR NIGHT SHARING THE HURTS AND WOUNDS WE HAD IMPOSED UPON EACH OTHER, WHETHER INTENTIONAL OR UNINTENTIONAL. THAT NIGHT WE DECIDED THAT AS CHRISTIANS WE DID NOT WISH TO BECOME ANOTHER DIVORCE STATISTIC AND THAT WE WOULD WORK WITH THE LORD'S HELP TO DEVELOP A HEALTHY MARRIAGE. I BEGAN TO PRAY EVEN HARDER THAT GOD WOULD RESTORE MY LOVE FOR MY HUSBAND.

GOD BEGAN A WORK IN BOTH OF US THAT NIGHT. IT WAS SO AMAZING TO SEE HIM AT WORK BEHIND THE SCENES. I REMEMBER, FOR EXAMPLE, HEARING A SERMON ON LOVE PREACHED AT OUR CHURCH ONE SUNDAY MORNING AND THE FOLLOWING SUNDAY AS WE VISITED MY SISTER'S CHURCH IN ANOTHER STATE, ALMOST THE SAME SERMON WAS PREACHED BY HER PASTOR. THAT MAKES ONE BEGIN TO THINK THAT GOD IS TRYING TO GET A POINT ACROSS WHEN YOU HEAR TWO ALMOST IDENTICAL MESSAGES ONE WEEK AFTER ANOTHER.

I MUST SAY THAT OUR MARRIAGE WAS NOT HEALED OVERNIGHT, NOR WAS OUR LOVE RESTORED IMMEDIATELY. HOWEVER, WE BEGAN TO TAKE DAILY LONG WALKS TOGETHER WHICH FORCED US TO TALK WITH EACH OTHER. WITHIN A YEAR, OUR SPARK OF LOVE WAS REKINDLED.

TODAY AS WE HAVE GROWN MORE DEEPLY IN LOVE, WITH EACH PASSING YEAR, IT IS HARD TO BELIEVE THAT WE HAD GONE THROUGH SUCH A DIFFICULT TIME...ONE OF ALMOST THROWING IN THE TOWEL AND HAVING OUR MARRIAGE TO END IN DIVORCE. IT'S AMAZING TO SEE THE TRANSFORMATION GOD HAS DONE IN BOTH OF US.

I OFTEN WONDER HOW MANY MARRIAGES COULD BE SPARED IF BOTH PARTNERS WOULD BE WILLING TO PRAY, SEEK GOD'S FACE AND STRIVE TO PUT THE OTHER SPOUSE BEFORE THEMSELVES.

I AM THANKFUL THAT GOD DID ALLOW US TO GO THROUGH THIS VALLEY. IT HAS ENABLED US TO SHARE WITH OTHER STRUGGLING

COUPLES THAT THERE IS HOPE, IF ONLY WE'LL TURN TO GOD FOR HELP!

"DO NOTHING FROM SELFISHNESS OR EMPTY CONCEIT, BUT WITH HUMILITY OF MIND LET EACH OF YOU REGARD ONE ANOTHER AS MORE IMPORTANT THAN HIMSELF." PHILIPPIANS 2:3 (NEW AMERICAN STANDARD BIBLE)

CHAPTER EIGHT

A CALLING FROM GOD

DID YOU KNOW THAT GOD HAS A PLAN FOR YOUR LIFE? AS FAR AS THAT GOES, HE HAS A SPECIAL PLAN FOR EVERYONE'S EXISTENCE. HOWEVER, FEAR CAN ROB US OF GOD'S BEST PLAN FOR OUR LIVES, IF WE ARE NOT CAREFUL. IT ALMOST HAPPENED TO ME.

WHEN I WAS IN MY EARLY FORTIES, MY TWO CHILDREN WERE BOTH IN SCHOOL, AND LIFE WAS GOING PRETTY SMOOTHLY. ALL OF A SUDDEN THINGS TOOK A TURN FOR THE WORSE. OUR CHRISTIAN SCHOOL WHERE I HAD TAUGHT WAS ABRUPLY CLOSED AT THE END OF THE YEAR DUE TO FINANCIAL PROBLEMS. I BECAME SUDDENLY UNEMPLOYED... I NEEDED TO WORK, NOT BECAUSE I WANTED TO, BUT BECAUSE OUR

TIGHT BUDGET DEMANDED IT! I WAS DETERMINED TO FIND WORK BY FALL, SO ALL SUMMER I FOUND MYSELF KNOCKING ON DOORS AND FILLING OUT RESUMES, WITHOUT HARVESTING ANY RESULTS. THIS WAS THE FIRST TIME IN MY LIFE THAT I HAD FILLED OUT APPLICATIONS AND PURSUED A JOB. PREVIOUSLY, IN MY WORKING CAREER, I HAD ALWAYS BEEN APPROACHED AND ASKED TO ACCEPT POSITIONS; THIS WAS DEFINITELY THE LEADING OF GOD FOR MY LIFE'S PATH.

FALL WAS APPROACHING. MEANWHILE, WE RELOCATED OUR HOME CLOSER TO A NEW POSITION MY HUSBAND HAD ACCEPTED. THIS ALSO INVOLVED OUR CHANGING TO A NEW PLACE OF WORSHIP. APPROXIMATELY A YEAR LATER, WE DECIDED IT WOULD BE TO OUR ADVANTAGE TO MOVE OUR MEMBERSHIP TO THIS NEWER CHURCH CLOSER TO OUR NEW HOME.

THE FOLLOWING TUESDAY AFTER WE JOINED THE NEW CHURCH, I DECIDED TO ATTEND A BIBLE STUDY LUNCHEON TO BECOME BETTER ACQUAINTED WITH MY NEW SISTERS IN

CHRIST. WHILE GOING THROUGH THE LINE TO FILL MY PLATE WITH THE WONDERFUL DELICACIES, I HEARD SOMEONE WHISPER MY NAME. WHEN I LOOKED BACK TO SEVERAL BEHIND ME, I NOTICED THE PASTOR' S WIFE WHISPERING TO HER HUSBAND. AS I FINISHED THE BUFFET LINE AND SCURRIED TO FIND A GOOD SEAT, THE PASTOR CAME UP, TAPPED ME ON THE SHOULDER AND ASKED IF I COULD MEET WITH HIM IN HIS OFFICE AS SOON AS I FINISHED MY LUNCH. I HAD A DIFFICULT TIME DIGESTING MY FOOD, AS I BEGAN TO IMAGINE ALL KINDS OF THOUGHTS. PERHAPS AFTER SEEING MY FULL PLATE, HE WAS GOING TO SPEAK TO ME ABOUT GLUTTONY! EVEN WORSE, HE MIGHT CANCEL OUR NEW MEMBERSHIP TO THE CHURCH! I JUST COULDN'T IMAGINE WHAT IN THE WORLD HE WOULD WANT TO SEE ME ABOUT.

AFTER WIPING THE LAST MORSEL FROM MY LIPS, I RELUCTANTLY WENT TO HIS OFFICE, KNOCKED ON HIS DOOR, AND WENT IN AT HIS BIDDING. HIS OLDER, GENTLE FACE SHOWED NO CONDEMNATION OF MY FOOD INTAKE, BUT INSTEAD OFFERED A

REQUEST FOR ME TO CONSIDER PRAYING ABOUT. I WAS TOLD IN CONFIDENCE THAT THE CURRENT CHILDREN'S MINISTER WAS BEING TRANSFERRED TO ANOTHER STATE. HE WANTED ME TO PRAY ABOUT TAKING HER POSITION! UNKNOWN TO ME AT THAT TIME, AS HE WAS PRAYING ABOUT THE REPLACEMENT, MY FACE HAD COME TO HIS MIND. ALTHOUGH HE DID NOT KNOW MUCH ABOUT ME AND WAS EVEN UNFAMILIAR WITH MY NAME, HE FELT AS IF GOD WAS LEADING HIM TO APPROACH ME ABOUT THIS REQUEST. HE ASK ME TO PRAY FOR TWO WEEKS AND THEN TO GET BACK WITH HIM. I COULD HAVE TOLD HIM RIGHT THEN THAT THE POSITION WAS NOT FOR ME. AFTER ALL, THE CHURCH, WHICH BOASTED A LARGE MEMBERSHIP, HOSTED AN EXTREMELY FAST GROWING CHILDREN'S MINISTRY. IT INVOLVED A SPECIAL MONTHLY SUNDAY NIGHT CHILDREN'S SERVICE, WHICH WOULD REQUIRE ME TO SPEAK BEFORE THIS GIGANTIC CONGREGATION. NO WAY!! I WAS HORRIFIED TO SPEAK TO ANY GROUP LARGER THAN TEN...ESPECIALLY BIG PEOPLE. I DID HOWEVER PROMISE TO PRAY ABOUT IT.

ALTHOUGH MY HEART WAS NOT REALLY IN IT, I WAS HONEST AND REMAINED FAITHFUL TO PRAY. I TALKED WITH MY HUSBAND AND PERSUADED HIM TO AGREE WITH ME THAT IT WAS A MUCH TOO DIFFICULT TASK TO ATTEMPT. I JUST DIDN'T FEEL CAPABLE OR QUALIFIED. AFTER TWO WEEKS I MET WITH THE PASTOR, TOLD HIM THAT I WAS A SUBMISSIVE WIFE, AND THAT MY HUSBAND AND I BOTH FELT IT WOULD BE TOO MUCH FOR ME. WITH THAT BEING SAID, I WALKED OUT THE DOOR. AS THE DOOR CLOSED BEHIND ME, ONE WOULD HAVE THOUGHT THAT I WOULD HAVE FELT AS "FREE AS A BIRD", BUT NOT SO! IT SEEMED I HAD GRIEVED THE HOLY SPIRIT AND FELT AS IF I HAD LET MY PRECIOUS SAVIOR DOWN.

I HAVE NEVER HEARD THE VOICE OF THE LORD AUDIBLY AS SOME HAVE; HOWEVER, THE FOLLOWING SUNDAY AS I WAS PREPARING FOR CHURCH, I HAD THE STRONGEST THOUGHT TO RUN THROUGH MY MIND AND SEEMED TO TAKE LODGING THERE. "GO IN AND POSSESS THE LAND!" IT CAME LOUD AND CLEAR. I WAS ALARMED AT FIRST, AND AFTER PONDERING

THE THOUGHT FOR A WHILE, WONDERED IF THIS WAS GOD SPEAKING TO MY HEART, TELLING ME TO GO IN AND POSSESS THAT POSITION OF CHILDREN'S MINISTER. I IMMEDIATELY THOUGHT OF THE TEN SPIES WHO WERE SENT INTO CANAAN LAND AND ONLY TWO, JOSHUA AND CALEB, CAME BACK WITH POSITIVE REPORTS. WAS I ONE OF THE NEGATIVE SPIES WHO PROCLAIMED IT COULDN'T BE DONE? ALL I COULD SEE WERE BIG GIANTS IN THE LAND CALLED ADULTS. I SUDDENLY BECAME REALLY BRAVE AND ASKED THE LORD TO CONFIRM IF INDEED IT WAS HIM SPEAKING TO ME TO ACCEPT THE POSITION.

THAT SUNDAY NIGHT I ARRIVED AT CHURCH EARLY AND WAS IN THE CAR, READING A BOOK SOMEONE HAD GIVEN ME ON OVERCOMING THE BONDAGE OF FEAR. THAT WAS EXACTLY WHAT I WAS DEALING WITH...FEAR. FEAR OF PEOPLE, BIG PEOPLE, BIG GIANTS, CALLED ADULTS! I NOTICED WHEN I LOOKED AT MY WATCH, IT WAS ALMOST TIME FOR CHURCH SERVICE TO BEGIN. I DECIDED TO GLANCE AT THE NEXT FEW PAGES TO DETERMINE IF I

HAD ENOUGH TIME TO FINISH THE CHAPTER. TO MY UTTER AMAZEMENT, THERE ON THE FOLLOWING PAGE WAS THE NEXT SECTION IN LARGE CAPTIONS ENTITLTED, "HOW TO GO IN AND POSSESS THE LAND!" INSTEAD OF SAYING "THANK YOU LORD FOR SEND-ING THIS CONFIRMATION," I SIGHED AND BREATHED, "LORD, PLEASE LET THIS BE A COINCIDENCE." I RESOLVED TO RECEIVE ANOTHER CONFIRMATION FROM THE LORD BEFORE I MADE ANY DECISION CONTRARY TO MY WILL! ALTHOUGH I HAD MY "SPIRITUAL EARPHONES" ON, I DID NOT RECEIVE ANOTHER WORD FROM GOD THAT NIGHT.

THE NEXT MORNING, FEELING VERY PERPLEXED, I CALLED MY SISTER WHO LIVED IN A NEIGHBORING STATE TO GET HER OPINION ON WHAT I SHOULD DO ABOUT THIS IMPORTANT DECISION. AGAIN TO MY ASTONISHMENT, INSTEAD OF EMPATHIZING WITH ME, SHE SHARED THAT HER DEVOTIONAL THAT VERY MORNING WAS ABOUT GOING IN TO POSSESS THE LAND! I HUNG UP THE PHONE AND GRABBED SOME TISSUES TO DRY MY WET EYES.

THE NEXT SUNDAY, AS WE ATTENDED SUNDAY SCHOOL FOR THE FIRST TIME AT THE NEW CHURCH, WE WERE LED UP THE STEPS, PAST THE CHILDREN MINISTER'S OFFICE AND INTO THE NEW CLASS WE SHOULD BE ATTENDING. YOU WILL NOT GUESS WHAT THE TOPIC WAS FOR THAT DAY. YES, YOU ARE CORRECT. IT WAS "GOING IN TO POSSESS THE LAND!"

AS I LEFT THAT CLASS, I KNEW, BEYOND A SHADOW OF A DOUBT, THAT I WAS TRULY BEING CALLED BY GOD TO GO IN AND POSSESS THE LAND WITH THAT POSITION. I MET WITH THE PASTOR AND TOLD HIM HOW I FELT THE LORD HAD BEEN LEADING ME AND OF HOW INCAPABLE I FELT. HE WAS SYPATHETIC, BUT ENCOURAGED ME THAT THE LORD WOULD NEVER CALL ME TO DO SOMETHING UNLESS HE EQUIPPED ME TO ACCOMPLISH THE TASK.

IT SEEMED AS SOON AS I HAD CONSENTED TO ACCEPT THE POSITION, EVERY TIME I TURNED ON THE RADIO OR READ AN ARTICLE, THE SUBJECT WOULD CONSIST OF GOING IN TO POSSESS THE LAND! I IMAGINED I HAD RECEIVED 365 CONFIRMATIONS, OR AT LEAST

IT SEEMED THAT WAY TO ME! I WAS STILL RELUCTANT AND TORN IN MY SPIRIT. ON ONE SIDE, IT SEEMED MY MIND WOULD ARGUE, "HANG IT UP BEFORE YOU MAKE A FOOL OF YOURSELF." ON THE OTHER SIDE WOULD COME THE THOUGHT, "I CAN DO ALL THINGS THROUGH CHRIST WHO STRENGTHENS ME!" IT WAS A CONSTANT BATTLE BACK AND FORTH.

THE FRIDAY BEFORE I WAS GOING TO BE INTRODUCED ON SUNDAY AS THE NEW CHILDREN'S PASTOR, I WAS TOTALLY EXHAUSTED SPIRITUALLY, EMOTIONALLY, AND PHYSICALLY FROM THE BATTLE THAT HAD BEEN RAGING WITHIN ME. FOR YEARS I HAD PRACTICED THE HABIT OF BEGINNING MY DAY BY READING GOD'S WORD. ALTHOUGH I HAD ALREADY READ MY BIBLE THAT MORNING, TODAY I FELT I NEEDED TO HAVE MY FAITH RENEWED. I KNEW THAT RENEWAL WOULD COME THROUGH THE READING OF GOD'S WORD. I DID NOT DARE TO ASK FOR ANOTHER CONFIRMATION. HE HAD BEEN SO GRACIOUS TIME AFTER TIME TO GIVE ME HIS LEADING THROUGH THIS DECISION. I DECIDED JUST

TO OPEN MY BIBLE AND BEGIN READING. IT FELL OPEN TO DEUTERONOMY ELEVENTH CHAPTER. I COULD HARDLY BELIEVE WHAT I WAS READING! THE ENTIRE CHAPTER WAS NOT ABOUT POSSIBLY CROSSING OVER... IT WAS A DEFINITE MANDATE OF GOING IN TO POSSESS THE LAND AND OF HOW HE WAS GOING TO GO BEFORE ME! I BROKE DOWN AND PROFUSELY WEPT. I TOLD THE LORD THAT IT DID NOT MATTER TO ME IF I GOT UP ON THAT STAGE AND HAD TWO OR THREE NERVOUS BREAKDOWNS IN FRONT OF EVERYONE; I WOULD SERVE HIM, HOWEVER HE WISHED, BECAUSE I LOVED HIM SO MUCH AND WANTED TO PLEASE HIM BY MY OBEDIENCE.

I SERVED AS CHILDREN'S MINISTER FOR THIRTEEN YEARS AND CAN TRUTHFULLY SAY THAT THIS WAS THE MOST INSPIRING AND REWARDING THING I HAVE EVER DONE IN MY LIFE. TO SEE CHILDREN GIVE THEIR HEARTS TO JESUS WHEN THEY ARE YOUNG AND TENDER, TO SEE THEM GROW IN HIS GRACE AND LEARN TO FOLLOW HIM IN OBEDIENCE IS ONE OF THE MOST HEARTFELT PLEASURES

OF LIFE. I AM SO GLAD ALSO THAT I DID NOT FEEL CAPABLE OF WORKING IN THIS CAPACITY BECAUSE IT FORCED ME TO RELY TOTALLY ON HIS STRENGTH, RATHER THAN MINE. IN DOING SO, HE RECEIVED ALL OF THE GLORY RATHER THAN ME. I PRAISE HIM THAT HE DID NOT GIVE UP ON ME AND CHOOSE SOMEONE ELSE TO DO THE WORK HE HAD FOR ME! I'VE LEARNED THAT HE USES ORDINARY PEOPLE TO DO HIS EXTRORDINARY WORK!

"I CAN DO ALL THINGS THROUGH CHRIST WHO STRENGTHENS ME". PHILIPPIANS 4:13 (KING JAMES BIBLE)

CHAPTER NINE

PROPHECIES COME TRUE

THE DATE WAS A SPECIAL DAY, MARCH TWENTY-SECOND. I REMEMBER IT WELL BECAUSE IT WAS MY BIRTHDAY. I WAS LOOKING FORWARD TO MY HUSBAND TAKING ME OUT FOR A SPECIAL BIRTHDAY MEAL THAT NIGHT AFTER WORK.

FRIENDS OF OURS, WHO WERE MISSIONARIES, WERE HERE IN AMERICA RAISING FUNDS FOR THEIR MINISTRY IN BRAZIL. HER COUSIN AND SPOUSE WERE BOTH EMPLOYED AS CHILDRENS' MINISTERS AND WERE VISITING FROM PENNSYLVANIA. MY FRIEND CALLED TO SEE IF SHE COULD DROP THEM OFF AT MY OFFICE TO DISCUSS THE WORK OF CHILDREN'S MINISTRIES. I ASSURED HER THAT I WOULD WELCOME THAT OPPORTUNITY TO SHARE

OUR COMMON PASSION. I QUICKLY FINISHED THE WORK I WAS DOING AND WAS READY TO MEET WHEN THEY ARRIVED.

WE ENJOYED SUCH AN ENRICHING TIME OF FELLOWSHIP AND LEARNED MUCH AS WE SHARED OUR BARRAGE OF IDEAS. WHEN IT WAS TIME FOR THEM TO LEAVE, THEY ASKED IF THEY COULD PRAY OVER ME. I ENCOURAGED THEM TO FEEL FREE. I FELT LIKE I NEEDED ALL THE PRAYERS I COULD GET!

AS THEY FINISHED PRAYING, THE HUSBAND PROPHESIED TWO THINGS OVER ME. A PROPHECY HAD NEVER BEEN SPOKEN OVER ME, SO I WAS A NOVICE. ALTHOUGH I WEPT AS THEY PRAYED AND PROPHESIED, I WAS THINKING TO MYSELF, "THIS IS WAY OFF IN LEFT FIELD!" FIRST, HE DECLARED THAT I WOULD BE USED OF THE LORD BY THE END OF THE YEAR IN A FOREIGN FIELD SHARING JESUS WITH CHILDREN. I HAD NO DESIRE TO GO ON A MISSION TRIP, SO I KNEW THIS WAS OFF BASE. SECONDLY, HE PROCLAIMED THAT A RELATIONSHIP WOULD BE RESTORED BEFORE THE YEAR WAS UP. AGAIN, I KNEW HE WAS

WRONG, BECAUSE I HAD ALWAYS REFRAINED FROM HOLDING ANIMOSITY TOWARD ANYONE AND NO ONE, TO MY KNOWLEDGE, WAS AGAINST ME. AS A MATTER OF FACT, ONE OF THE SCRIPTURES I HAD ALWAYS ADHERED TO WAS, "LET NOT THE SUN GO DOWN UPON YOUR WRATH." (EPHESIANS 4:26)

NEVER ONCE HAD I GONE TO BED ANGRY AT ANYONE...NOT EVEN MY HUSBAND. WE HAD ALWAYS MADE AMMENDS BEFORE RETIRING FOR THE NIGHT! I DIDN'T TELL THE GENTLEMAN WHO PROPHESIED THAT HE WAS WRONG; I JUST KNEW IN MY MIND THAT HE WAS! I TUCKED IT ALL AWAY IN MY HEART, FORGOT ABOUT WHAT HE HAD SAID, AND WENT ON THAT DAY ENJOYING MY BIRTHDAY.

SEVERAL MONTHS PASSED AND I HAD NOT GIVEN THOSE PROPHECIES A SECOND THOUGHT. AS THE MONTH OF OCTOBER APPROACHED ALONG WITH THE COLOR CHANGE OF FOLIAGE, I WAS ON MY WAY TO WORK ONE DAY WITH THE RADIO BLARING AS USUAL. MY MIND CAME TO ATTENTION

WHEN I HEARD THE ANNOUNCEMENT THAT VOLUNTEERS WERE NEEDED FOR A MISSION TRIP TO DISTRIBUTE CHRISTMAS PACKAGES AND TELL CHILDREN ABOUT JESUS. SOMETHING IN MY HEART LEAPED AND I BECAME SO EXCITED. THE RADIO ANNOUNCEMENT WAS COMING FROM OKLAHOMA AND A PHONE NUMBER WAS GIVEN TO FIND OUT THE DETAILS. DRIVING ALONG THE ROAD, THERE IN VIRGINIA, I SCRAMBLED TO FIND A PEN AND QUICKLY WROTE DOWN THE NUMBER.

AS I CAME IN THROUGH THE CHURCH OFFICE DOORS TO GREET THE SECRETARY, WHEN SHE ASKED HOW I WAS DOING, I EXCITEDLY EXCLAIMED THAT I WAS GOING ON A MISSION TRIP! WHEN SHE ASKED WHEN AND WHERE, I COMMENTED THAT I DIDN'T KNOW. I HAD TO CALL FOR THE DETAILS, BUT I JUST KNEW I WAS GOING! WHEN I DID CALL TO INQUIRE, I DISCOVERED THAT WE WOULD BE TRAVELING TO COSTA RICA AND I WOULD NEED TO FURNISH MY OWN TRAVELING EXPENSE OF $1200! I DID NOT HAVE $1200 TO SPARE SO I FELT A LITTLE DISAPPOINTED. I

PROBABLY THOUGHT THAT MY WAY WOULD BE PAID BY WHOEVER WAS SPONSORING THE TRIP. BUT NOT SO; EVERY PENNY HAD TO BE PAID BY THOSE ATTENDING. WHAT DID I KNOW ANYWAY? I HAD NEVER BEEN ON A MISSION TRIP BEFORE.

THE THOUGHTS OF A FUND-RAISER DID NOT ENTER MY MIND. HOWEVER, GOD ENABLED ME TO PEN A BEAUTIFUL HOUSE BLESSING POEM, WHICH HAD BEEN MATTED AND FRAMED FOR MY NEICE'S NEW HOME DEDICATION. WHEN I SHOWED IT TO MY BEST FRIEND, SHE WANTED TO PURCHASE ONE JUST LIKE IT. I TOLD HER THAT I COULD NOT SELL HER ONE. I KNEW IT HAD BEEN GIVEN TO ME BY GOD, AND I DID NOT WANT TO CHARGE MONEY FOR HIS GIFT. WHEN SHE STATED THAT SHE DID NOT WANT ONE UNLESS SHE COULD PAY FOR IT, THE THOUGHT CAME TO ME TO ACCEPT A LOVE OFFERING FOR THE FRAMED WORK AS PAYMENT TOWARD MY MISSION TRIP. NEXT THING I KNEW, I HAD ORDERS FOR MORE THAN I COULD HANDLE! MY TOTAL MISSION FEE OF $1200 PLUS $50 EXTRA HAD COME IN WITHIN A WEEK AND

HALF. WHEN GOD PLANS SOMETHING FOR YOUR LIFE, HE MAKES PROVISIONS FOR IT TO BE CARRIED OUT!

ALTHOUGH I HAD NOT THOUGHT OF THE FIRST PROPHECY AS BEING FULFILLED, IT CAME TO PASS DURING THE MONTH OF NOVEMBER.

REGARDING THE SECOND PROPHECY, THIS ALSO CAME TO FRUITION. I HAD A FIRST COUSIN WHO WAS EXTREMELY CLOSE-- ALMOST LIKE A SISTER. ALTHOUGH WE LIVED ABOUT 500 MILES FROM EACH OTHER, WE KEPT CLOSE COMMUNICATION TWO OR THREE TIMES EACH WEEK. AFTER RETURNING FROM MY MISSION TRIP, I REALIZED THAT HER PHONE CALLS WERE BECOMING LESS FREQUENT. EVENTUALLY, IT GOT TO THE POINT THAT SHE NEVER CALLED ANYMORE. I WAS THE ONE WHO INITIATED THE CALLS; HOWEVER, SHE ALWAYS WAS FRIENDLY TOWARD ME. I E-MAILED HER ONE DAY AND INQUIRED IF SHE WAS MAD AT ME ABOUT SOMETHING…SHE NEVER CALLED ANYMORE. A FEW DAYS LATER, SHE E-MAILED BACK WITH

A RESPONSE THAT LEFT ME DEVASTATED. SHE TOLD ME THAT SHE HOPED NEVER TO SEE ME AGAIN. I HAD CORRECTED HER ABOUT SOMETHING AND SHE HAD BEEN HIGHLY OFFENDED. INSTEAD OF INFORMING ME OF THE OFFENSE, SHE HAD BECOME ANGRY AND ALLOWED HATRED TO HARBOR. I ENDED UP WRITING APPROXIMATELY THREE PAGES OF APOLOGY ASKING FOR FORGIVENESS. I ASSURED HER OF MY LOVE AND ENLIGHTENED HER OF MY APPRECIATION OF HER FRIENDSHIP. I EXPRESSED THAT SHE COULD CHOOSE TO HATE ME IF SHE WISHED, BUT I CHOSE TO LOVE HER REGARDLESS. SHE HAD BEEN SO WONDERFUL TO MY HUSBAND AND ME DURING OUR EARLY YEARS OF MARRIAGE. SHE AND HER HUSBAND EVEN SHARED THEIR HOME WITH US ONE SUMMER UNTIL WE COULD FIND HOUSING. I WOULD NEVER FORGET HER KINDNESS AND WOULD CONTINUE TO LOVE HER FOR IT.

CHRISTMAS CAME AND WENT QUICKLY. SOON AFTER, I SURPRISINGLY RECEIVED A LETTER OF APOLOGY FROM MY COUSIN. SHE, BEING AN ONLY CHILD, HAD GONE THROUGH SO

MUCH WITH THE AGING AND PASSING OF HER PARENTS, A DIVORCE OF A DAUGHTER AND MANY OTHER TRIALS. SHE JUST COULD NOT HANDLE IT ALL. SHE EXPRESSED HOW SHE WANTED TO FORGET WHAT HAD HAPPENED AND WANTED TO BEGIN ANEW WITH OUR RELATIONSHIP. I WAS MORE THAN PLEASED TO ACCEPT HER APOLOGY.

THE POSTMARK DATE OF THE LETTER... DECEMBER THIRTIETH! THE LAST DAY OF THAT YEAR!

IT WAS NOT UNTIL FEBRUARY, ALMOST A YEAR LATER THAT I REALIZED THAT BOTH PROPHECIES SPOKEN OVER ME HAD COME TO FRUITION. IT IS DIFFICULT TO ALWAYS SEE THINGS IN THE SPIRITUAL REALM WITH OUR PHYSICAL HEARTS EYES.

"NOW WE SEE THINGS IMPERFECTLY AS IN A CLOUDY MIRROR, BUT THEN WE WILL SEE EVERYTHING WITH PERFECT CLARITY. ALL THAT I KNOW NOW IS PARTIAL AND INCOMPLETE, BUT THEN I WILL KNOW EVERYTHING COMPLETELY, JUST AS GOD NOW

KNOWS ME COMPLETELY." 1 CORINTHIANS 13:12 (NEW LIVING TRANSLATION)

"DO NOT STIFLE THE HOLY SPIRIT. DO NOT SCOFF AT PROPHECIES, BUT TEST EVERYTHING THAT IS SAID. HOLD ON TO WHAT IS GOOD." I THESSALONIANS 5:19-20 (NLT)

CHAPTER TEN

EMPTIED AND FILLED UP

WHILE WORKING AS CHILDRENS' PASTOR, WORD HAD SPREAD THAT A GREAT REVIVAL WAS HAPPENING IN BROWNSVILLE, FLORIDA. AS A MATTER OF FACT, THE REVIVAL STARTED ON FATHER'S DAY AND CONTINUED SEVERAL YEARS.

MY PRAYER PARTNER, CONNIE, DISCOVERED THAT A LARGE NEIGHBORING CHURCH WAS TO BE TAKING A BUS LOAD OF HUNGRY SOULS TO ATTEND, AND INVITED ME TO COME AS HER ROOMMATE. I HAD NO INTEREST WHATSOEVER. SHE WAS RATHER PERSISTENT THOUGH AND ENCOURAGED ME TO GO. AS GOD WOULD HAVE IT, MY HUSBAND THOUGHT IT WAS A WONDERFUL IDEA AND MIRACULOUSLY, THE EXACT AMOUNT OF

MONEY NEEDED FOR TRANSPORTATION AND EXPENSES WAS PROVIDED. SO OFF WE WENT. I WAS NOT SO EXCITED, BUT RATHER WAS VERY APPREHENSIVE. WHAT IF I GOT INTO GOD'S PRESENCE AND HE SHOWED HIS DISPLEASURE IN ME? AS FAR AS I WAS CONCERNED, ALL OF MY SINS WERE UNDER THE BLOOD; BUT IF THE ACCOUNTS I HAD HEARD WERE ACCURATE, IT WAS A SCARY THING TO SEE GOD'S PRESENCE MANIFESTED.

ONCE WE REACHED OUR DESTINATION, WE STOPPED FOR OUR EVENING MEAL, A BIG BUFFET IN WHICH I COULD INDULGE IN MY FAVORITE DESSERT, CHEESECAKE! FROM THERE WE SETTLED IN FOR THE NIGHT AT OUR MOTEL. THE NEXT MORNING, WE HURRIEDLY ATE BREAKFAST AND WENT TO GET IN THE WAITING LINE WHICH WOULD ENABLE US TO BE ASSURED OF A SEAT FOR THAT EVENING'S SERVICE. WE HAD HEARD THAT THE CHURCH'S LIGHTS WERE CUT OFF AND DOORS WERE LOCKED AT MIDNIGHT... WITH PEOPLE WHO ATTENDED THAT NIGHT'S SERVICE, COMING OUT, TO GET IN LINE TO REMAIN ALL DAY FOR THE FOLLOWING

EVENING'S SERVICE! WOW! WHEN OUR BUS ARRIVED EARLY THAT MORNING, I COULD HARDLY BELIEVE THE LONG LINE ALREADY ASSEMBLED OUTSIDE THE CHURCH. PEOPLE WERE WAITING PATIENTLY FOR THE DOORS TO BE OPENED AT SIX PM FOR THE EVENING SERVICE.

THE LONG DAY OF STANDING IN THE SUN SEEMED TO PASS RATHER QUICKLY AS WE ALL CONVERSED WITH EACH OTHER. FINALLY THE DOORS WERE OPENED, AND I COULD NOW ACKNOWLEDGE THAT THE RUMORS I HAD HEARD ABOUT THE GREAT REVIVAL WERE ABSOLUTELY TRUE! I WAS SO HUNGRY FOR MORE OF GOD, THAT BY THE TIME THE ALTAR WAS OPENED FOR PRAYER, I ALMOST RAN DOWN THE AISLE. I WAS SO DESIROUS OF THE PRESENCE OF GOD IN MY LIFE, I FOUND MYSELF DOWN AT THE FRONT, BEGGING TO BE PRAYED OVER. I DID RECEIVE A TOUCH FROM GOD THAT NIGHT AS I EMPTIED MY HEART TO HIM. I HARDLY KNOW HOW TO DESCRIBE IT OTHER THAN STREAKS OF ELECTRICITY HITTING MY SOUL AND FLOWING THROUGHOUT MY BODY. I COULD

NOT REMAIN STILL, BUT CONTINUOUSLY QUAKED IN HIS PRESENCE! I UNDERSTAND NOW WHY THE CHRISTIANS OF OLD WERE NAMED "QUAKERS". THAT NIGHT AS THE LIGHTS WERE TURNED OUT AND THE DOORS OF THE CHURCH WERE LOCKED, I WAS SO DRUNK ON THE NEW WINE OF THE HOLY SPIRIT, THAT I HAD NO IDEA AS TO HOW I GOT BACK TO MY MOTEL ROOM. I JUST REMEMBER COLLAPSING ON THE BED AND "QUAKING" ALL NIGHT IN HIS PRESENCE, NOT EVEN TAKING THE TIME TO CHANGE INTO PAJAMAS OR BRUSH MY TEETH.

THE NEXT MORNING I AROSE WITHOUT EATING BREAKFAST AND RETURNED TO THE CHURCH TO SPEND THE MORNING IN A CLASS ON INTERCESSORY PRAYER. AS I SAT IN THAT CLASSROOM, I FELT I NEEDED TO GET OUT OF THERE AND FIND A PRIVATE MEETING PLACE WITH THE LORD. WHEN I COULD NO LONGER RESIST, I QUICKLY WENT OUTSIDE. I THOUGHT PERHAPS I COULD EVEN FIND A RESTROOM WHERE I COULD BE ALONE TO WORSHIP GOD IN ONE OF THE STALLS. I DID NOT MAKE IT TO A RESTROOM, HOWEVER. I FOUND A

SET OF STEPS OUTSIDE OF A BUILDING AND COLLAPSED THERE WORSHIPING HIM AND HAVING MY OWN LITTLE REVIVAL IN HIS PRESENCE. I HAVE NO IDEA HOW LONG I WAS THERE BEFORE MY ROOMMATE AND SOME OTHER FRIENDS FOUND AND INFORMED ME THAT IT WAS TIME FOR OUR GROUP TO GO BACK TO THE BUFFET RESTAURANT TO EAT. I WAS NOT HUNGRY AND DID NOT DESIRE TO GO. THEY REMINDED ME THAT I HAD NOT EATEN SINCE THE DAY BEFORE AND INSISTED ON HELPING ME ONTO THE BUS. RELUCTANTLY, I CLIMBED ON AND FOUND A SEAT. BEFORE THE BUS TOOK OFF, IT SEEMED AS IF THE VOICE OF THE LORD ASKED ME, "WOULD YOU RATHER GO BACK AND EAT MORE OF THAT CHEESECAKE, OR STAY HERE AND PARTAKE OF THE MILK AND HONEY I AM FEEDING YOU?" WITH THAT IN MIND, I TOLD MY ROOMMATE THAT I COULD NOT GO WITH THE GROUP. I WAS GOING TO STAY BEHIND AND CONTINUE MY COMMUNION WITH THE LORD. SHE DECIDED THAT SHE WOULD STAY WITH ME.

WE FOUND A SHADE TREE AND SAT UNDER IT AS I WROTE THE THINGS THE LORD WAS SPEAKING WITH ME ABOUT. CONNIE AND I DID NOT VERBALLY COMMUNICATE. I GUESS YOU COULD SAY THAT MY HEAD WAS IN THE HEAVENLIES. I WILL FOREVER BE GRATEFUL FOR A FRIEND LIKE CONNIE WHO SACRIFICED TO STAY BEHIND WITH ME, YET WAS WILLING NOT TO INTERFERE WITH MY TIME WITH THE LORD.

WHEN I RETURNED HOME, I WAS A CHANGED PERSON. BECAUSE OF MY QUAKING THAT FIRST NIGHT, I WAS SO CONCERNED ABOUT WAKING MY HUSBAND. TO KEEP FROM DISTURBING HIS SLEEP, I LITERALLY GOT OUT OF BED AND FELL ON MY KNEES BEFORE GOD. THAT QUAKING SENSATION WAS WITH ME FOR A LONG PERIOD OF TIME, PERHAPS TWO OR THREE WEEKS. I HAVE NO IDEA WHAT IT WAS ALL ABOUT, UNLESS GOD WAS JUST PURGING AND SHAKING IMPURITIES FROM MY SOUL. I DO KNOW THAT THE SPIRIT OF THE LIVING GOD IS REAL!

BROWNSVILLE TRIP NUMBER TWO!

UPON OUR RETURN FROM THE TRIP TO BROWNSVILLE REVIVAL, OUR SENIOR PASTOR ALLOWED BOTH CONNIE AND ME TO SHARE OUR EXPERIENCES DURING THAT SUNDAY NIGHT'S SERVICE. OUR EXCITEMENT OF WHAT GOD HAD DONE FOR US SPILLED OVER RESULTING IN SEVERAL PEOPLE REQUESTING THAT I GET A TRIP TOGETHER FOR THEM. THE LORD WORKED OUT DETAILS FOR US TO RENT A NEW BUS. WITH ABOUT TWENTY FIVE ATTENDEES, OFF WE WENT. THIS TIME MY HUSBAND WAS ABLE TO ACCOMPANY US! AMONG THE TRAVELERS WERE TWO OTHER MEN, WHO WERE WORKERS IN THE BOYS DEPARTMENT. I WAS THRILLED THEY WERE GOING. ONE WAS AN OLDER, BIG, TALL GUY WHO ALWAYS WORE A COWBOY HAT AND BOOTS.

I NOTICED THE FIRST NIGHT OF OUR ATTENDANCE IN THE REVIVAL, BOTH MEN HAD "PERCHED" THEMSELVES IN THE BALCONY AS SPECTATORS. I LATER SEARCHED THEM OUT AND PRIVATELY TALKED WITH

THEM. I TOLD THEM THAT WE HAD TRAVELED
APPROXIMATELY THIRTEEN HOURS AND IF
THEY CHOSE TO SIT AND ONLY SPECTATE,
THAT WAS THEIR OWN BUSINESS; HOWEVER,
IF THEY WISHED TO RECEIVE ANYTHING
FROM THE LORD, I RECOMMENDED THAT
THEY GO DOWN FOR PRAYER WHENEVER THE
INVITATION WAS GIVEN. I ALSO INSTRUCTED
THE ENTIRE GROUP TO MEET THAT NIGHT AT
THE BUS NO LATER THAN MIDNIGHT SHARP.
THE CHURCH WOULD BE CLEARING OUT BY
THEN TO LOCK THE DOORS, AND WE WOULD
EMBARK OUR LONG TRIP BACK TO VIRGINIA.

MIDNIGHT ARRIVED QUICKLY AND EVERYONE
WAS ACCOUNTED FOR WITH THE EXCEPTION
OF THE BIG, TALL TEXAN-LOOKING GUY.
AFTER WAITING ABOUT FIFTEEN MINUTES
AND RECOUNTING HEADS, I WAS BEGINNING
TO BE CONCERNED. AS MY HUSBAND AND I
WERE GETTING OFF THE BUS TO LOOK FOR
OUR MISSING SHEEP, I SAW IN THE DISTANCE,
SOMEONE PUSHING A WHEELCHAIR WITH
OUR BIG GUY SITTING SLUMPED PARTIALLY
OVER. AS HE APPROACHED AND WAS BEING
HELPED UP THE STEPS OF THE BUS, HE

INCESSANTLY APOLOGIZED FOR BEING LATE.
HIS SLURRED SPEECH INDICATED THAT HE
WAS DRUNK, BUT NOT WITH ALCOHOL! HE
WAS "DRUNK IN THE SPIRIT" WITH NEW WINE
POURED OUT BY THE HOLY SPIRIT!!! HE HAD
YIELDED TO GOD AND WAS FILLED UP TO
OVERFLOWING…A CHANGED MAN FOREVER!

IT WAS HUMOROUS WHEN THE BUS
DRIVER'S WIFE, WHO WAS NOT PART OF OUR
CONGREGATION, QUESTIONED IF THE MAN
WAS ALRIGHT. I TOLD HER THAT HE WAS FINE
AND THAT HE HAD JUST INDULDGED IN TOO
MUCH TO DRINK!

"AND BE NOT DRUNK WITH WINE, WHEREIN
IS EXCESS; BUT BE FILLED WITH THE SPIRIT;"
EPHESIANS 5:18 (KJV)

CHAPTER ELEVEN

THE MYSTERY OF THE MISSING DIAMONDS

I ALWAYS PROUDLY WORE MY WEDDING RING, THE SYMBOL THAT I WAS MARRIED UNTIL "DEATH DO US PART." THE DIAMOND WAS NOT VERY LARGE, NOT EVEN ONE HALF CARAT IN SIZE. YET I REALIZED HOW HARD MY HUSBAND HAD WORKED ALL SUMMER TO PURCHASE THE RING BEFORE HE PROPOSED. TO MAKE SURE IT WAS FREE OF FLAWS, HE HAD EVEN STUDIED THE DIAMOND AND INSPECTED IT WITH THE JEWELER'S MAGNIFIER.

I HAD ENJOYED WEARING THE RING AT LEAST THIRTY YEARS OR MORE, WHEN AN INCIDENT OCCURRED THAT REALLY DISTURBED ME. I WAS DRIVING HOME ONE DAY AFTER WORK

WHEN I STOPPED FOR A RED LIGHT. MY EYE CASUALLY GLANCED AT THE SIGHT OF AN EMPTY ENCASMENT HEAD WHERE MY DIAMOND HAD BEEN. "OH," I THOUGHT, "IF I DON'T FIND THIS MISSING DIAMOND, I HAD BETTER FIX A REALLY GOOD MEAL FOR HUBBY BEFORE I BREAK THE NEWS!" TO MY DISMAY, THE DIAMOND WAS NOT FOUND. AFTER WE FINISHED EATING A DELICIOUS DINNER, I BROKE THE NEWS. I WAS SURPRISED AT HIS REACTION. HE SIMPLY REMARKED, "I SUPPOSE GOD FELT LIKE YOU WERE FINISHED WITH IT." NONETHELESS, WE DID PRAY TOGETHER THAT NIGHT THAT THE MISSING JEWEL WOULD BE FOUND. WE CONTINUED TO PRAY AS WE SEARCHED FRANTICALLY FOR THE TREASURE. AFTER A COUPLE OF WEEKS OF PRAYING AND SEARCHING, I GAVE UP. SINCE IT WAS LIKE FINDING A NEEDLE IN A HAYSTACK, I CONCLUDED THAT IT WOULD BE AN ABSOLUTE MIRACLE TO FIND THE LOST STONE. MY FAITH HAD DWINDLED TO ZERO. HOWEVER, MY HUSBAND, AFTER PRAYING FOR A COUPLE OF WEEKS, ONE MORNING FELT REPENTANT OF HIS FAILURE TO BELIEVE THAT

GOD COULD FIND IT. HE ASKED THE LORD TO HELP HIS UNBELIEF AS HE REPENTED.

THAT DAY AT WORK, OUR STAFF WENT OUT TO CELEBRATE A CO-WORKER'S BIRTHDAY. UPON OUR RETURN, WHEN THE SECRETARY UNLOCKED HER OFFICE DOOR, I WENT IN TO CHECK MY WORK BOX. THIS WAS ROUTINE TO SEE IF I HAD ANY FINISHED WORK TO BE RETRIEVED. I HAD CHECKED MY WORKBOX AT LEAST TEN TO TWELVE TIMES SINCE MY DIAMOND HAD BEEN LOST. MY POSITION AS CHILDREN'S MINISTER REQUIRED THE SECRETARY TO COMPLETE MORE WORK FOR MY DEPARTMENT THAN ANY OTHER DIVISION. SHE ALWAYS PLACED THE COMPLETED WORK IN MY WORKBOX FOR ME TO PICK UP. I FOUND NO COMPLETED WORK THAT DAY--ONLY SOMETHING SHINY GLISTENING IN THE LIGHT! I CAREFULLY PICKED IT UP, WRAPPED IT IN A TISSUE AND TUCKED IT AWAY. I SUSPECTED THAT ONE OF MY CO-WORKERS HAD ATTEMPTED TO PLAY A TRICK BY PLACING A FAKE ZERCONIA IN MY WORKBOX. WE WERE ALWAYS TEASING EACH OTHER. I INQUIRED, BUT EACH ONE PROMISED

ME THEY DID NOT KNOW ANYTHING ABOUT IT. I IMMEDIATELY TOOK IT TO A JEWELER AFTER WORK. HE CONFIRMED THAT IT WAS A TRUE DIAMOND. AND JUST AS FASCINATING WAS THE FACT THAT IT FIT PERFECTLY INTO THE PRONGS OF MY WEDDING RING!

I AM STILL IN QUESTION AS TO HOW IT SUDDENLY APPEARED IN THE MIDDLE OF MY WORK BOX AFTER BEING LOST FOR TWO WEEKS. AGAIN, MY WORKBOX HAD BEEN CHECKED SEVERAL TIMES DURING THOSE TWO WEEKS. MY CO-WORKERS SUGGESTED THAT PERHAPS IT HAD BEEN "HAND DELIVERED" BY AN ANGEL. REGARDLESS OF HOW IT GOT THERE, I AM GRATEFULLY PLEASED AND THANKFUL.

"IMMEDIATELY THE BOY'S FATHER CRIED OUT AND BEGAN SAYING, 'I DO BELIEVE; HELP MY UNBELIEF." MARK 9:24 (NEW AMERICAN STANDARD BIBLE)

SECOND MYSTERY OF MISSING DIAMOND

IN FEBRUARY OF 2006, MY HUSBAND SURPRIZED ME BY HAVING MY DIAMOND REMOUNTED INTO THE CENTER OF A BEAUTIFUL CLUSTER SURROUNDED BY SMALLER DIAMONDS. HE PRESENTED ME WITH THE NEW RING GUARD ON VALENTINE'S DAY AS A TOKEN OF LOVE. WE DECIDED TO HAVE THE COMPLETE RING SOLDERED TOGETHER SO IT COULD BE WORN WITH EASE.

THREE MONTHS LATER WE MADE OUR MINI MOVE FROM WILMINGTON TO ENJOY OUR SEASON AT THE SMOKY MOUNTAIN CABIN. WE HAD SETTLED INTO OUR DWELLING PLACE WHEN I WAS ASKED TO ASSIST MY SISTER-IN-LAW BY DRIVING HER TO AN APPOINTMENT AT THE OPTHAMOLOGIST. HER FAILING EYESIGHT HAD PUT A HALT TO HER DRIVING ABILITY.

ONCE WE GOT TO THE DOCTOR'S OFFICE, I BEGAN TO FILL OUT HER PAPER WORK, WHEN ALL OF A SUDDEN, I NOTICED MY ORIGINAL

DIAMOND WAS MISSING FROM THE CENTER OF THE CLUSTER. I ABRUPTLY PUT MY PEN DOWN AND FRANTICALLY BEGAN LOOKING ON THE FLOOR, UNDER THE DESK AND EVERYWHERE I THOUGHT IT MIGHT BE. SOME OF THE KIND PEOPLE IN THE OFFICE SAW MY CONCERN AND BEGAN ALSO LOOKING, BUT TO NO AVAIL. AS SOON AS I COMPLETED THE PAPER WORK, AND SITUATED MY SISTER-IN-LAW, I EXITED TO SEARCH THE CAR, PARKING AREA AND SIDEWALK, RETRACING MY EVERY STEP.

ALTHOUGH MUCH PRAYER WENT UP CONCERNING THE MISSING JEWEL, THE DIAMOND WAS NOT FOUND. MY HUSBAND FINALLY DECIDED TO PURCHASE A LOOSE DIAMOND TO REPLACE THE MISSING ONE. OTHERWISE, THE RING COULD NOT BE WORN. I JOKINGLY ACCUSED HIM OF BEING CONCERNED THAT SOME GENTLEMAN MIGHT FLIRT WITH ME, THINKING I WAS A SINGLE GAL, SINCE I WAS NOT WEARING A WEDDING RING.

SPRING QUICKLY TURNED TO THE HEAT OF SUMMER AND THEN AN ARRAY OF FALL

COLORS BEGAN TO APPEAR. OCTOBER BROUGHT THE PEAK OF COLORS TO THE MOUNTAINS.

ONE BRISK OCTOBER MORNING, WE HAD COMPLETED OUR COFFEE AND DEVOTIONS AND I BEGAN TO CLEAR THE TABLE FOR BREAKFAST. I HAPPENED TO SEE A TINY OBJECT OFF TO ONE SIDE. AT FIRST I THOUGHT IT WAS A RHINESTONE. BEING LOCATED IN THE SAME AREA WHERE DOLLY PARTON HAD GROWN UP, I ENJOYED THE "GLITZIE" LOOK AS WELL AND THOUGHT PERHAPS I HAD LOST ONE OF MY FAKE DIAMONDS FROM A BRACELET OR SOME PIECE OF COSTUME JEWELRY. HOWEVER, WITH CLOSER EXAMINATION, I DECIDED IT LOOKED "REAL." I WRAPPED THE TINY TREASURE IN TISSUE AND TOOK IT TO THE LOCAL JEWELER WHO CONFIRMED THAT IT WAS A REAL DIAMOND!

THOUGHTS CAME ABOUT DOING SOMETHING SPECIAL FOR MY HUSBAND LIKE HAVING A BAND MADE WITH THE DIAMOND. HOWEVER, WHEN I THOUGHT ABOUT THE FACT THAT HE HAD ALREADY LOST TWO WEDDING BANDS,

I DECIDED TO DO SOMETHING SELFISHLY DIFFERENT. I ENDED UP HAVING MY ORIGINAL, TWICE LOST DIAMOND, SECURELY PLACED AT THE TIP OF MY FAVORITE PENDANT.

MANY TIMES I HAVE PONDERED WHAT A MIRACLE IT WAS FOR MY MISSING DIAMOND TO REAPPEAR NOT ONCE, BUT TWICE! THE SECOND TIME, MY PRECIOUS STONE WAS LOST A TOTAL OF SIX MONTHS, FROM MAY UNTIL OCTOBER. THE STRANGE FACT WAS THAT WE HAD EATEN AT, AND CLEANED THAT LITTLE BREAKFAST TABLE MANY TIMES DURING THAT SIX MONTH PERIOD. I, TO THIS DAY, HAVE NOT FIGURED THAT ONE OUT!

OFTEN I HAVE THOUGHT OF THE LESSON RECEIVED THROUGH THE TWO MYSTERIES. I HAVE COME TO THE CONCLUSION THAT REGARDLESS OF HOW FAR WE ROAM FROM THE LORD, HE IS ABLE TO FIND US.

"OR WHAT WOMAN, IF SHE HAS TEN SILVER COINS AND LOSES ONE COIN, DOES SHE NOT LIGHT A LAMP AND SWEEP THE HOUSE AND SEARCH CAREFULLY UNTIL SHE FINDS IT?"

"AND WHEN SHE HAS FOUND IT, SHE CALLS TOGETHER HER FRIENDS AND NEIGHBORS SAYING, 'REJOICE WITH ME, FOR I HAVE FOUND THE COIN WHICH I HAD LOST!'

"IN THE SAME WAY, I TELL YOU, THERE IS JOY IN THE PRESENCE OF THE ANGELS OF GOD OVER ONE SINNER WHO REPENTS." LUKE 15:8-10 (NEW AMERICAN STANDARD BIBLE)

CHAPTER TWELVE

CAROLINA, HERE WE COME!!

FOR YEARS WE HAD TALKED ABOUT MOVING TO WILMINGTON, NORTH CAROLINA, TO BE CLOSE TO MY OLDER SISTER AND BROTHER-IN-LAW. WE HAD ALWAYS ENJOYED A CLOSE RELATIONSHIP SPIRITUALLY AND THOROUGHLY CHERISHED THEIR FRIENDSHIP AS WELL. APPARENTLY, EACH TIME WE MADE AN ATTEMPT TO MOVE, IT WAS NOT GOD'S PERFECT TIMING. DO YOU EVER FEEL AS IF HIS TIME CLOCK IS NOT SYNCHRONIZED WITH YOURS? AFTER SEVERAL ATTEMPTS, WE FINALLY GAVE UP.

FOLLOWING MY HUSBAND'S EARLY RETIREMENT, WE BECAME INVOLVED WITH ESTABLISHING A NEW CHURCH IN WILLIAMSBURG, VIRGINIA. IT WAS A QUICK

GROWING, CONTEMPORARY CHURCH WHICH WAS CONSIDERED A "PORTABLE CHURCH". IT WAS FACILITATED IN A RENTED MIDDLE SCHOOL BUILDING AND NEEDED TO BE "SET UP" WEEKLY. WE CERTAINLY HAD FUN ARRIVING EXTREMELY EARLY AND STAYING LATE TO "SET UP" AND "BREAK UP CAMP" WEEKLY.

ONE SUNDAY NIGHT WE WERE GOING OUT THE DOOR TO A NEIGHBORHOOD BIBLE STUDY AT ONE OF THE CHURCH FAMILY'S HOME, WHEN THE PHONE RANG. IT WAS MY SISTER'S DAILY CALL. BEFORE HANGING UP, SHE MADE THE COMMENT, "NOW REMEMBER, IF ANYONE SAYS ANYTHING ABOUT MOVING TO NORTH CAROLINA WITHOUT YOU BRINGING UP THE TOPIC, YOU MAY AS WELL BEGIN PACKING YOUR BAGS." I MENTIONED IT TO MY HUSBAND AS WE WALKED ALONG TO OUR NEIGHBOR'S HOUSE AND HE THOUGHT IT WAS AMUSING.

AFTER THE BIBLE STUDY, WE WERE ENJOYING SOME LIGHT REFRESHMENTS AND FELLOWSHIP.

I MENTIONED TO ONE OF THE LADIES WITH WHOM I WAS CHATTING HOW MUCH I WAS ENJOYING THE MUSIC. USUALLY IT WAS SO LOUD, I WOULD HAVE HAD TO TURN MY HEARING AIDS OFF (IF I REALLY HAD SOME), BUT LATELY, IT SEEMED AS IF THE MUSIC HAD BEEN TUNED "JUST RIGHT." THE LADY COMMENTED TO ME THAT I HAD BETTER ENJOY IT WHILE IT LASTED, BECAUSE THE YOUNG MAN ON THE KEYBOARD WAS GETTING READY TO MOVE TO CAROLINA! I NUDGED MY HUSBAND AND WE BOTH SMILED. SHE THEN ASKED, "WHAT IS SO FUNNY ABOUT THAT?" I RESPONDED WHAT MY SISTER HAD RELATED TO ME VIA PHONE JUST BEFORE WE LEFT OUR HOUSE. "OH, SO THAT MEANS YOU ARE GOING TO MOVE TO CAROLINA?" SHE QUIPPED. "NOT NECESSARILY," I QUICKLY RETORTED. "THE BIBLE STATES, "OUT OF THE MOUTH OF TWO OR MORE WITNESSES A FACT WILL BE ESTABLISHED." ON THE WALK HOME I TOLD MY HUSBAND THAT A GOOD CONFIRMATION FROM GOD WOULD BE IF WE HAD SOMEONE APPROACH US ABOUT SELLING OUR HOUSE, WITHOUT US TAKING THE INITIATIVE. THAT INCIDENT HAD NEVER HAPPENED BEFORE.

NO MORE WAS MENTIONED THAT NIGHT ABOUT MOVING.

SOON THEREAFTER, WE LEFT THE AREA FOR A SIX WEEKS STAY AT OUR SMOKY MOUNTAIN CABIN WE HAD INHERITED. IT WAS AN INTENSE, DREADED CHORE MAKING ARRANGEMENTS TO HAVE OUR MAIL COLLECTED, HOUSE PLANTS WATERED OCCASSIONALLY, AND THE HOUSE CHECKED ON PERIODICALLY. IT WAS REALLY WORTH THE EFFORT HOWEVER, TO BE ABLE TO ENJOY RELAXING IN OUR LITTLE MOUNTAIN CABIN SURROUNDED BY BEAUTIFUL AUTUMN COLORS.

UPON OUR RETURN TO VIRGINIA, WE WERE INUNDATED WITH A STACK OF MAIL... MOST OF IT JUNK. ONE OF THE HANDWRITTEN ENVELOPES WHICH CAUGHT OUR ATTENTION ENCLOSED A BEAUTIFUL CARD WITH A SCRIPTURE VERSE ON THE FRONT. INSIDE WAS A HANDWRITTEN NOTE FROM A FRIEND I HAD NOT HEARD FROM NOR TALKED WITH IN A COUPLE OF YEARS. SHE INFORMED US THAT SHE HAD BECOME

A LICENSED REALTOR AND SAID SHE JUST THOUGHT OF US AND WISHED TO SELL OUR HOME IF WE EVER DECIDED TO RELOCATE. MY HUSBAND WAS GETTING READY TO TOSS IT INTO FILE THIRTEEN WITH THE OTHER JUNK MAIL, WHEN I ABRUPTLY STOPPED HIM. I EXCLAIMED, "JAY, THAT SOUNDS LIKE THE CONFIRMATION FROM GOD THAT WE HAVE BEEN WAITING FOR!" HE RESPONDED THAT THOUGHT HAD NOT EVEN CROSSED HIS MIND. HE DID MENTION THAT HE WOULD RATHER TRY SELLING OUR HOUSE OURSELVES RATHER THAN GOING THROUGH A REALTOR. WE WOULD BUY A "FOR SALE" SIGN AS SOON AS WE COULD GET THE HOUSE IN TIP-TOP SHAPE.

GETTING OUR HOUSE READY AND OUR FOR SALE SIGN IN THE YARD CAME QUICKLY AND SO DID THE BUYER. WITHIN THIRTY DAYS OUR HOUSE WAS UNDER CONTRACT WHICH MEANT A QUICK TRIP TO LOOK FOR A NEW HOUSE IN WILMINGTON! WE HAD JUST SIX WEEKS TO PACK AND GET OUT!

FINDING A NEW HOUSE WAS NOT SO SIMPLE.
AFTER THREE DAYS OF FRUITLESS EXERTION
WE WERE READY TO GIVE UP. WE DECIDED
THAT FINDING ONE WITHIN OUR BUDGET
WAS NEXT TO IMPOSSIBLE. WHILE WE WERE
PRAYING FOR GUIDANCE, MY SISTER ON THE
FOURTH DAY TOLD US THAT WE MIGHT
FIND ONE WE LIKED AT THE CAPE. WHEN I
ASKED ABOUT THE CAPE, SHE TOLD ME THAT
IT WAS A BEAUTIFUL GATED SUBDIVISION.
WE DROVE OUT TO TAKE A LOOK, BUT
THERE AGAIN, HOUSE AFTER HOUSE WITH
"FOR SALE" SIGNS IN THE YARDS WERE WAY
OVERPRICED FOR OUR BUDGET. AS WE DROVE
INTO THE LAST CUL-DE-SAC BEFORE LEAVING
THE SUBDIVISION, WE NOTICED A NICE ONE
STORY, NOT SO EXTRAVAGANT HOUSE FOR
SALE. ALTHOUGH IT HAD A REALTOR'S SIGN
IN THE YARD, I DECIDED TO KNOCK ON THE
DOOR TO SEE IF WE COULD TAKE A QUICK
LOOK WITHOUT AN APPOINTMENT. TO MY
SURPRIZE, A COUNTRY SOUNDING LADY
CAME TO THE DOOR AND TOLD US THAT SHE
WOULD BE DELIGHTED TO HAVE US LOOK. SHE
SOUNDED COUNTRY JUST LIKE US BECAUSE
SHE WAS ORIGINALLY FROM KNOXVILLE,

TENNESSEE, NOT FAR FROM WHERE OUR MOUNTAIN CABIN WAS LOCATED.

WHEN I STEPPED INSIDE, MY HEART LEAPED! THE HOUSE WAS BEAUTIFULLY DECORATED, JUST THE WAY I LIKED IT. THERE WAS NOTHING I WOULD NEED TO CHANGE! AFTER STROLLING THROUGH EVERY ROOM AND OOHING AND AAHING OVER THE DECORATIONS, WE DECIDED TO MAKE AN OFFER. WE KNEW THE LISTED PRICE AND OUR OFFER WAS MUCH, MUCH LOWER. MY HUSBAND WAS HESITANT, STATING THAT THEY MIGHT JUST LAUGH US OFF, BUT MY BROTHER-IN-LAW WHO HAD ONCE WORKED AS A REALTOR HIMSELF ENCOURAGED HIM BY STATING THAT ALL THEY COULD DO IS SAY NO. MY HUSBAND THEN MADE THE OFFER AND HE WAS RIGHT... THEY LAUGHED. WE DECIDED TO COUNTER OFFER AND AFTER MANY HOURS OF NEGOTIATING BACK AND FORTH, A DEAL WAS FINALLY BIRTHED! THE SALE WAS WITHIN $2000 OF OUR ORIGINAL OFFER, WITH THE PREREQUISITE OF THEIR LEAVING THE REFRIGERATOR IN THE HOUSE (WHICH WAS AT LEAST A $1500 ITEM). I WAS

SO EXCITED AND FELT ALMOST AS IF A NEW BABY HAD BEEN BORN, SINCE WE HAD BEEN IN SO MUCH LABOR THROUGHOUT THE NEGOTIATION TRANSACTIONS.

ON SATURDAY MORNING WHEN DEPARTURE TIME CAME, I WAS SO EXCITED AND GRATEFUL FOR OUR NEW HOME, BUT STILL LONGED TO BE ASSURED THAT THIS WAS THE RIGHT HOUSE. I SENT UP A QUICK PRAYER FOR CONFIRMATION TO THE LORD. I ALSO MADE A CALL TO THE SELLER TO SEE IF WE COULD STOP BY ON OUR WAY OUT TO MAKE PICTURES OF THE HOUSE. I DIDN'T TRUST MY MEMORY IN THE EVENT I FOUND CURTAINS, ETC. TO BE PURCHASED FOR OUR NEW PLACE. SHE WELCOMED US WARMLY. WHEN WE ARRIVED, ONE OF THE FIRST THINGS SHE TOLD ME WAS THAT SHE HAD FAILED TO MENTION THAT THEY HAD A DOG NAMED JAY THEY HOPED WOULD GO ALONG WITH THE SALE OF THE HOUSE. I JOKINGLY BUT EMPHATICALLY REPLIED, "THANKS, BUT NO THANKS, ONE JAY IN THE HOUSE IS ENOUGH!"

SHE THEN PROCEEDED TO TAKE ME OUT TO THE FRONT LAWN AND INTRODUCED ME TO THE NEIGHBORS, ALTHOUGH NONE WERE AROUND IN PERSON, ONLY IN SPIRIT. SHE INFORMED ME THAT THE OLDER COUPLE ACROSS THE STREET WERE GORDON (MY BROTHER'S NAME) AND MILLIE. NEXT DOOR LIVED BOB (MY BROTHER-IN-LAW'S NAME) AND BARBARA (MY SISTER-IN- LAW'S NAME) AND ON AND ON. WITHIN THAT LITTLE SHORT CUL-DE-SAC LIVED PEOPLE WITH SEVEN OF MY FAMILY'S NAME! GOD'S PERFECT NUMBER! I TOOK IT AS AN AMAZING CON-FIRMATION THAT THIS INDEED WAS THE HOUSE GOD HAD SELECTED FOR US!

THE BLESSINGS DID NOT STOP THERE. WHEN WE ARRIVED BACK IN VIRGINIA TO BEGIN OUR PACKING, A MILITARY FAMILY HAD MOVED ACROSS THE STREET FROM US. HE KNOCKED ON OUR DOOR AND OFFERED US ALL OF HIS MOVING BOXES. HE HAD LEARNED FROM SOME OF THE NEIGHBORS THAT WE WERE MOVING. THIS WOULD SAVE US A GREAT EXPENCE, THANKS TO UNCLE SAM AND THIS NEW NEIGHBOR'S THOUGHTFULNESS!

AFTERNOTE:

THE COUPLE FROM WHOM WE PURCHASED OUR WILMINGTON HOUSE WERE ON THEIR BOAT TWO WEEKS AFTER THE MOVE WHEN THE HUSBAND HAD A SEIZURE. HE WAS DIAGNOSED WITH A BRAIN TUMOR AND SUFFERED FOR ALMOST A YEAR BEFORE HE DIED. I AM SO THANKFUL TO REPORT THAT DURING THAT YEAR OF SUFFERING, HE BEGAN ATTENDING A CHURCH AND SURRENDERED HIS HEART TO JESUS BEFORE PASSING AWAY.

A TESTIMONY OF HOW GOD ALLOWED ME TO MINISTER TO THE WIFE OF THE DYING MAN FOLLOWS IN THIS BOOK. WE PRAYED MUCH FOR HIS SALVATION WHEN WE LEARNED OF HIS ILLNESS.

"TRUST IN THE LORD WITH ALL YOUR HEART, AND DO NOT DEPEND ON YOUR OWN UNDERSTANDING. SEEK HIM IN ALL YOU DO, AND HE SHOW YOU WHICH PATH TO TAKE."

PROVERBS 3:5-6 (NLT)

CHAPTER THIRTEEN

SMOKY MOUNTAIN RAIN (OR SNOW) KEEPS ON CALLING (OR FALLING)!

I GUESS WE COULD BE CLASSIFIED AS SNOWBIRDS. SPENDING THE SUMMER MONTHS AT OUR LITTLE FOUR ROOM SMOKY MOUNTAIN CABIN WAS PRETTY REFRESHING-- UNTIL THE YEAR OF 2006. THAT PARTICULAR YEAR WE BEGAN OUR PILGRIMAGE SOON AFTER THANKSGIVING BACK TO WILMINGTON FOR THE WINTER MONTHS. CELEBRATING ALL OF THE THINGS WE HAD TO BE THANKFUL FOR, WE ALWAYS ENJOYED THAT SPECIAL HOLIDAY WITH MY HUSBAND'S FAMILY.

WE RESEMBLED THE BEVERLY HILLBILLIES CROSSING THE MOUNTAIN RANGE OF ASHEVILLE, NORTH CAROLINA. I LED THE CAROVAN WITH MY VECHICLE LOADED TO THE MAX AND MY HUSBAND FOLLOWED NEXT IN THE PARADE LOADED DOWN AS WELL. EACH SEASON WAS LITERALLY LIKE A MINI MOVE BACK AND FORTH, FROM THE COASTAL SHORES OF NORTH CAROLINA TO THE MOUNTAINS OF TENNESSEE. WE ENJOYED THE VARIETY OF GOD'S HANDIWORK IN THE TWO OPPOSITE TERRAINIAL TOPOGRAPHIES. THIS PARTICULAR TRIP WAS NOT SUCH A PLEASANT EXPERIENCE, HOWEVER. SNOWFLAKES, SEEMINGLY THE SIZE OF QUARTERS, WERE COMING DOWN SO HEAVY THAT OUR VISION WAS BEING IMPAIRED. ALONG WITH MY NERVES, THE HIGHWAYS WERE QUICKLY BECOMING HAZARDOUS AS WELL. HOPING SOME REST WOULD ENABLE US TO WEATHER THE STORM ON TO OUR DESTINATION, WE STOPPED TO SPEND THE NIGHT. EVEN THIS BRIEF RESPITE DID NOT ALLEVIATE OUR STRESSFUL DRIVE THE REMAINDER OF OUR TRIP. WHEN WE FINALLY ARRIVED HOME TOTALLY EXHAUSTED, I TOLD MY HUSBAND

THAT I WAS GETTING TOO OLD FOR SUCH FUTURE TRIPS...I DIDN'T THINK MY NERVES WOULD EVER TAKE ANOTHER EPISODE LIKE THE ONE WE JUST HAD EXPERIENCED.

THE FOLLOWING SPRING WHEN WE ARRIVED AT OUR MOUNTAIN CABIN, WE BEGAN PRAYING THAT GOD WOULD LEAD AND GIVE US DIRECTION. WE LOVED OUR MOUNTAIN HOME AND WE ALSO LOVED WINTERING IN THE WARMER WEATHER OF WILMINGTON. WE WERE WILLING TO LIVE IN WILMINGTON YEAR ROUND AND WOULD BE SATISFIED JUST TO TAKE AN OCCASIONAL WEEK OR TWO VACATION TO THE CABIN. WE WERE ALSO WILLING TO SELL OUR HOME IN WILMINGTON AND MOVE PERMANENTLY TO THE MOUNTAINS. IT DID NOT REALLY MATTER TO US; WE JUST WANTED TO BE IN GOD'S PERFECT WILL.

WHILE AT THE CABIN, WE MADE PRAYING FOR GOD'S WILL A MATTER OF PRIORITY OUR ENTIRE STAY IN THE MOUNTAINS BEFORE HEADING BACK TO THE COAST THE FIRST OF DECEMBER. OUR HOT SUMMER

AND BEAUTIFULLY COLORED AUTUMN HAD CERTAINLY PASSED QUICKLY. THE FIRST OF DECEMBER I DECIDED TO ATTEND A BIBLE STUDY GROUP I HAD TAUGHT DURING MY PREVIOUS WILMINGTON WINTER STAY. MY HUSBAND WAS PLANNING TO MANICURE THE MUCH NEGLECTED SHRUBBARY AROUND THE HOUSE WHILE I WAS GONE. WHEN I ARRIVED HOME, HE INFORMED ME THAT A LADY HAD STOPPED TO INQUIRE WHO OWNED OUR HOUSE... SHE WAS INTERESTED IN BUYING IT. I THOUGHT HE WAS JUST KIDDING UNTIL HE FLIPPED OUT HER BUSINESS CARD. HE HAD TOLD HER THAT I WAS PRESENTLY NOT AT HOME BUT WOULD CALL TO HAVE HER COME OVER TO TAKE AN INSIDE TOUR OF THE HOUSE. SINCE THE HOUSECLEANING HAD BEEN DONE EARLIER, I IMMEDIATELY GAVE HER A QUICK CALL BEFORE SHE HAD TIME TO BACK OUT OF BEING INTERESTED. SHE CAME SOON AFTER AND SLOWLY MEANDERED FROM ROOM TO ROOM TAKING IN EVERY NOOK AND CRANNY. SHE ASKED US HOW MUCH WE WOULD TAKE FOR THE HOUSE. FROM THE TOP OF OUR HEADS POPPED AN ASTRONOMICAL FIGURE, ABOUT THIRTY THOUSAND DOLLARS MORE

THAN WE HAD PAID FOR IT. ALTHOUGH WE HAD PURCHASED THE HOUSE THREE YEARS EARLIER, WE HAD INHABITED IT ONLY EIGHTEEN MONTHS AND HAD DONE SOME MINOR UPGRADING. LATE THAT AFTERNOON SHE CAME BACK WITH A FIVE THOUSAND DOLLAR EARNEST MONEY DOWNPAYMENT WANTING TO KNOW WHEN WE COULD BE OUT! WE TOLD HER THAT WE WERE CHRISTIANS AND WE PRAYED ABOUT EVERYTHING. WE THOUGHT THAT SINCE GOD MIGHT BE IN THIS, HOWEVER, WE DID WISH TO HAVE UNTIL THE END OF DECEMBER TO PRAY AND MAKE SURE THIS WAS HIS DOINGS BEFORE MAKING A DEFINITE DECISION. UNKNOWN TO HER, WE ALSO DESIRED TO HAVE A MARKET ANALYSIS COMPLETED TO MAKE SURE NO ONE WOULD BE CHEATED. WE ACTUALLY HAD TWO MARKET ANALYSISES FIGURED AND DISCOVERED THAT WE WERE ON THE EXACT MARKET PRICE… COULD HAVE ASKED FOR EVEN MORE, HAD IT BEEN PUT IT INTO THE HANDS OF A REALTOR, BUT WE WOULD HAVE LOST THEIR SELLING FEE. AT THE END OF DECEMBER, WE MADE CONTACT WITH HER AND INFORMED THAT WE COULD BE OUT BY THE FIRST OF MARCH!

GOD WAS OUR REALTOR, SINCE WE NEVER HAD A CHANCE TO PUT UP A "FOR SALE" SIGN AND HAD NOT REALLY TALKED WITH ANYONE OTHER THAN HIM ABOUT SELLING IT! I HAVE LEARNED IN LIFE, THAT ALL ANSWERS TO PRAYERS ARE NOT SO EASILY AND QUICKLY REACHED; HOWEVER, IF WE PRAY FOR GOD'S WILL TO BE DONE IN OUR LIVES, AND GOD IS IN IT, HE WILL MAKE IT HAPPEN!

LOOKING BACK OVER OUR MOVE TO TENNESSEE, WE SOMETIMES SEE HINTS OF WHY GOD LED US HERE. I HAVE COME TO REALIZE TWO SPECIFIC REASONS. WE HAVE BEEN ABLE TO GIVE ASSISTANCE TO MY HUSBAND'S AGING SISTER WHO SUFFERED WITH ALZHEIMER'S DISEASE UNTIL HER DEATH. ALSO, HE HAS USED US, AS WELL AS GROWING US INTO SPIRITUAL MATURITY, AT THE CHURCH WE HAVE BEEN ATTENDING SINCE OUR RELOCATION.

"COMMIT YOUR ACTIONS TO THE LORD, AND YOUR PLANS WILL SUCCEED." PROVERBS 16:3 (NEW LIVING TRANSLATION)

II
LESSONS AND
PARABLES OF LIFE

NO FEAR OF COWS OR SATAN

HAVE YOU EVER BEEN CONSUMED WITH FEAR? I MEAN REALLY TERRIFIED OF SOMETHING? I SUPPOSE WE ALL HAVE LITTLE FEARS OF VARIOUS THINGS, WHETHER IT BE HEIGHTS, PUBLIC SPEAKING, MONSTERS (IS THERE SUCH A THING?) OR PEOPLE. I ONCE KNEW A WONDERFUL CHRISTIAN LADY WHO WAS HORRIFIED OF RIDING AN ELEVATOR. I ALSO HAVE A SISTER WHO WILL NOT FLY IN AN AIRPLANE FOR FEAR OF IT CRASHING. I ASSURRED HER ONCE THAT JESUS PROMISED HE WOULD BE WITH HER AND NEVER LEAVE HER. SHE QUICKLY REPLIED, "HE SAID LOW I AM WITH YOU ALWAYS!" APPARENTLY SHE DID NOT THINK THAT HE WOULD BE WITH HER HIGH IN THE AIR...ONLY LOW ON THE GROUND. AND WHAT ABOUT MY AUNT,

GROUNDED IN THE FAITH, WHO WAS FEARFUL OF PRAYING OUT LOUD IN PUBLIC. OH WELL, WHO KNOWS WHERE OUR FEAR COMES FROM OTHER THAN OUR ENEMY SATAN? HOWEVER, WE ALL KNOW THAT IT CERTAINLY IS THE OPPOSITE OF FAITH.

I USED TO BE FEARFUL OF COWS BELIEVE IT OR NOT. I GUESS THAT PHOBIA DERIVED FROM THE FACT THAT A BULL CAME RUNNING RAPACIOUSLY AFTER ME ONCE WHEN I WAS IN A PASTURE. MY SIBLINGS LAUGHED ABOUT IT AND SAID THAT THEY HAD NEVER SEEN ME RUN SO FAST! JUMPING THE BARBED WIRE FENCE, THEY ACTUALLY ACCUSED ME OF RESEMBLING AN OLYMPIC RUNNER!

THAT FEAR CONTINUED INTO MY ADULT LIFE. YEARS LATER WHEN MY HUSBAND AND I WOULD TAKE A SABBATICAL EACH SUMMER FROM OUR TEACHING CAREERS, TO WORK IN THE GREAT SMOKY MOUNTAINS TOURIST AREA, WE RESIDED IN AN OLD CABIN. THIS LITTLE DWELLING PLACE WAS ALMOST 200 YEARS OLD AND WAS SURROUNDED BY CATTLE WHICH GRAZED ON THE SURROUNDING

FARMLAND. ONE OF MY FAVORITE SPOTS OF THE LITTLE FOUR ROOM BUNGALOW WAS THE SCREENED IN FRONT PORCH. ON MY DAYS OFF FROM WORK, I COULD GET A FAVORITE BOOK, GRAB A GLASS OF ICED TEA AND RELAX IN THE SWING ON THAT PORCH FOR HOURS. I WAS DOING JUST THAT ONE DAY WHEN MY RELAXATION WAS INTERRUPTED WITH A LOUD STARTLING SOUND. I ALMOST JUMPED OUT OF MY SKIN WHEN I GLANCED UP FROM MY READING TO DISCOVER A COW STARING FEROCIOUSLY AT ME. IT MOOED LOUDLY AGAIN IN A THREATENING WAY. I WAS READY TO "RUN FOR COVER" WHEN IT DAWNED ON ME THAT THE COW COULD NOT "GET" ME BECAUSE I WAS PROTECTED BY THE SCREENED IN AREA. ALL OF A SUDDEN, I WAS NO LONGER AFRAID AND ACTUALLY BEGAN BRAVELY SINGING "NA, NANY BOO BOO, YOU CAN'T GET ME". A SPIRITUAL NUGGET IMMEDIATELY CAME TO MIND. SATAN THREATS US WITH HIS NOISE OF LOUD TAUNTS AND ACCUSATIONS, BUT HE CAN NOT REACH US BECAUSE WE ARE PROTECTED AND COVERED BY THE PRECIOUS BLOOD OF JESUS! NO MATTER HOW LOUD HE ROARS, WE NEED NOT FEAR HIM (OR COWS)

BECAUSE GREATER IS HE THAT IS IN US, THAN HE THAT IS IN THE WORLD! I'M REMINDED OF THAT OLD SONG, "SINCE JESUS KNOCKED HIS TEETH OUT, ALL HE CAN SAY IS MEOW-OW!"

"FOR GOD HATH NOT GIVEN US THE SPIRIT OF FEAR; BUT OF POWER, AND OF LOVE, AND OF A SOUND MIND." II TIMOTHY 1:7 (KINGS JAMES VERSION)

THE MYSTERIOUS PHONE NUMER

"CALL SHARON AND INVITE HER TO MEET FOR LUNCH." I HAD LEARNED TO RECOGNIZE THAT STILL SMALL VOICE. ALTHOUGH THE MESSAGE WAS LOUD AND CLEAR TO MY MIND, I KINEW I HAD CHORES TO COMPLETE BEFORE JOINING MY SISTER AND ANOTHER FRIEND FOR A LEISURELY BITE TO EAT. SHARON WAS AN ACQUAINTANCE FROM WHOM WE HAD PURCHASED OUR HOME IN WILMINGTON, NORTH CAROLINA. SHORTLY AFTER THE MOVE WAS FINALIZED, HER HUSBAND WAS DIAGNOSED WITH A BRAIN TUMOR. I RARELY EVER CALLED HER UNLESS I HAD A QUESTION RELATING TO THE HOUSE. "I'LL CALL AS SOON AS I FINISH VACUUMING," I THOUGHT.

LATER, WHILE DRIVING DOWN THE BACK ROAD TO MY LUNCHEON APPOINTMENT, MY THOUGHTS SUDDENLY AGAIN TURNED TO SHARON. I WAS REMORSEFUL THAT IN MY HASTE TO FINISH THE CHORES, I HAD FORGOTTEN TO CALL. I WAS TOTALLY UNFAMILIAR WITH HER NEW PHONE NUMBER, WHICH WAS TUCKED AWAY SECURELY AT HOME IN A DRAWER. I FELT COMPLETELY HELPLESS ABOUT GETTING IN TOUCH WITH HER NOW. AS I WAS ALREADY RUNNING A LITTLE LATE, I DID NOT HAVE TIME TO RETURN HOME TO RETRIEVE THE PHONE NUMBER. IF ONLY I HAD NOT PROCRASTINATED MAKING THAT CALL WHEN THE THOUGHT FIRST CAME TO ME. SUDDENLY A NUMBER FLASHED ACROSS MY MIND. I THOUGHT, WHY NOT TRY IT. I HAVE NOTHING TO LOSE. I CAN ALWAYS SAY, "SORRY, WRONG NUMBER," BEFORE HANGING UP. AFTER PULLING OVER, I REACHED FOR MY CELL PHONE AND QUICKLY DIALED THE NUMBER BEFORE IT HAD TIME TO EVAPORATE. I NEARLY DROPPED THE PHONE WHEN I HEARD SHARON'S VOICE ON THE OTHER END OF THE LINE. I HAD NEVER BEFORE OR

SINCE HAD ANYTHING LIKE THIS TO HAPPEN TO ME.

I NOW KNOW WHY GOD HAD BROUGHT THIS UNFAMILIAR PHONE NUMBER TO MY MIND. SHARON POURED OUT HER HEART OF ANXIETY AND HER DEFINITE NEED FOR BEING ENCOURAGED. SHE AND HER HUSBAND HAD JUST RETURNED FROM THE DOCTOR'S OFFICE AND FUNERAL HOME, HAVING BEEN TOLD TO MAKE ARRANGEMENTS FOR HER HUSBAND'S FINAL DAYS ON EARTH.

IT IS COMFORTING TO KNOW THAT WE SERVE A GOD WHO NOT ONLY KNOWS THE NUMBER OF HAIRS ON OUR HEADS, BUT IS FAMILIAR WITH OUR PHONE NUMBERS AS WELL!

"CALL TO ME, AND I WILL ANSWER YOU, AND I WILL TELL YOU GREAT AND MIGHTY THINGS, WHICH YOU DO NOT KNOW." JEREMIAH 33:3 (NEW AMERICAN STANDARD BIBLE)

THE SPECIAL VALENTINE GIFT

ANTICIPATION SURGED THROUGH ME AS I ANXIOUSLY TORE OPEN THE ENVELOPE. NEITHER THE USUAL VALENTINE CANDY NOR FLOWERS WERE ADORNING MY BREAKFAST TABLE THAT DREARY FEBRUARY FOURTEENTH MORNING. THE CARD, WHICH HAD BEEN LYING LIFELESS ON THE TABLE, I SURMISED WOULD BURST OPEN WITH LIFE AND MONEY TALKING--EXPRESSING A MESSAGE OF LOVE OF HOW MUCH I MEANT TO MY DEARLY BELOVED HUSBAND OF THIRTY TWO YEARS. HE HAD NEVER ONCE MISSED A SPECIAL OCCASION AS VALENTINES, BIRTHDAY, OR MOTHER'S DAY. AS I READ THE FRONT OF THE CARD AND CAUTIOUSLY OPENED TO THE INSIDE DARING ANY MONEY TO DROP OUT, I BECAME PUZZLED. NOTHING OTHER THAN AN "I

LOVE YOU HONEY MORE THAN EVER," NOTE DECORATED THE INSIDE. "THAT RASCAL," I THOUGHT. "HE IS PROBABLY BRINGING HOME A SURPRISE TONIGHT AFTER WORK. I GUESS I'LL JUST HAVE TO BE PATIENT."

THAT EVENING AS HE ARRIVED HOME, I MET HIM AT THE DOOR WITH A CHEERY KISS AND GREETING AWAITING MY SPECIAL GIFT PRESENTATION. AS THE EVENING WORE ON I BECAME MORE ANXIOUS ABOUT MY SURPRISE, AND FINALLY COULD WAIT NO LONGER. "HONEY, I APPRECIATED THE BEAUTIFUL VALENTINE CARD. NOW WHERE IS MY GIFT?" I INQUIRED. MY HUSBAND, UNUSUALLY QUIET, DID NOT RESPOND. I FINALLY BEGAN TO HASSLE HIM WITH A GAME OF SEARCHING HIS POCKETS WHILE GLEEFULLY ASKING, "DID YOU GET ME A RING OR PIECE OF JEWELRY?" MY IMAGINATION RAN WILD WITH ALL KINDS OF EXTRAVAGANT GIFTS RUNNING THROUGH MY THOUGHTS. MY HUSBAND JUST QUIETLY IGNORED MY QUESTIONS AS HE SHRUGGED AND STROLLED TO ANOTHER ROOM. TO MY UTTER AMAZEMENT NOTHING ELSE WAS MENTIONED THAT FATEFUL

DAY. DISAPPOINTMENT FILLED MY HEART. EVERYONE ELSE I KNEW WAS BEING PAMPERED WITH "I LOVE YOUS" AND THE "PROOF OF THE PUDDINGS" WAS THE GIFTS BEING BESTOWED. AS I TRUDGED DEJECTEDLY TO OUR BEDROOM, I REALIZED THAT ONE OF OUR FAVORITE SCRIPTURES WE HAD TAKEN GREAT PRIDE IN ADHERING TO THROUGHOUT THE YEARS OF OUR MARRIED LIFE WAS ABOUT TO BE VIOLATED… EPHESIANS 4:26, "LET NOT THE SUN GO DOWN UPON YOUR WRATH."

THE NEXT MORNING, THE FROWN ON MY USUAL SMILING FACE DECLARED THAT I WAS STILL HURT AND A LITTLE DISILLUSIONED. AS I CASUALLY BROUGHT THE SUBJECT UP ONCE AGAIN AT THE BREAKFAST TABLE, OUR SON, THE ONE WHO THOUGHT HE WAS THE EXPERT ON THE TOPIC OF LOVE, SUDDENLY CHIMED IN, "MOM, THERE IS YOUR VALENTINE GIFT." HE POINTED TO HIS DAD WHO WAS BEGINNING TO CLEAR THE DIRTY DISHES FROM THE TABLE WITHOUT EVEN BEING ASKED.

SUDDENLY IT DAWNED ON ME. IT WAS TRUE. I HAD FAILED TO RECOGNIZE THAT MY HUSBAND ALWAYS GAVE ME A VALENTINE'S DAY GIFT. NOT JUST ONE DESIGNATED DAY EACH YEAR, BUT EVERY SINGLE DAY OF THE YEAR. HE LAVISHED ME THROUGHOUT THE YEAR WITH KISSES, KIND WORDS, UNDERSTANDING, AND GENTLE TOUCHES. HE ALWAYS PITCHED IN TO HELP WITH THE HOUSEHOLD CHORES WITHOUT EVER BEING ASKED. I REALIZED THAT THIS WAS A GIFT FAR MORE PRECIOUS AND VALUABLE THAN A TEMPORAL GIFT GIVEN ON ONE SPECIAL DAY EACH YEAR WHICH WOULD SOON FADE AWAY. AS I GAVE HIM A BIG HUG AND A KISS, MY ANGER MELTED AWAY AS I PROCLAIMED, "I LOVE YOU FOR BEING MY SPECIAL VALENTINE GIFT!" AND I MEANT IT FROM THE VERY BOTTOM OF MY HEART.

"BE ANGRY, AND YET DO NOT SIN; DO NOT LET THE SUN GO DOWN ON YOUR ANGER." EPHESIANS 4:26 (NEW AMERICAN STANDARD BIBLE)

DON'T GIVE UP!

HAVE YOU EVER FELT DISCOURAGED, DEJECTED AND EVEN NEGLECTED BY THE LORD? RECENTLY, WHILE READING THE ACCOUNT OF THE GENTILE WOMAN WHO APPROACHED JESUS TO HEAL AND DELIVER HER DAUGHTER, I WAS AMAZED AT HER DETERMINATION. HER FIRST APPROACH INVOLVED HER CRYING OUT WITH A LOUD VOICE FOR HIM TO TOUCH HER DAUGHTER. IT SEEMED AS IF HE HAD NOT HEARD HER OR PERHAPS WAS JUST IGNORING, BECAUSE HE DID NOT ANSWER HER A WORD. HAD IT BEEN ME FEELING THE NEGLECT, I WOULD HAVE BEEN DISCOURAGED AND POSSIBLY GIVEN UP WITH THAT FIRST TRY.

IN ADDITION TO THIS SEEMINGLY REJECTION BY JESUS, THE DISCIPLES IMPLORED HIM TO SEND HER AWAY SINCE SHE WAS MAKING SUCH A DISTURBANCE. I WOULD FOR SURE HAVE LEFT THE SCENE, PROBABLY TELLING THE DISCIPLES WHAT I THOUGHT OF THEM. BUT NOT THIS LADY!

THIRDLY, JESUS FINALLY TOLD HER THAT HE WAS SENT ONLY TO THE LOST SHEEP OF ISRAEL, AND NOT TO THE DOGS. (MARK 7:27) I WOULD HAVE DEFINITELY TAKEN THIS AS AN INSULT, BUT AGAIN THIS LADY REACTED DIFFERENTLY. SHE WAS SO DESPERATE, SHE CAME, AND KNEELING, WORSHIPED HIM & KEPT PRAYING, "LORD, HELP ME!"

I BELIEVE JESUS WAS TRULY TESTING HER FAITH, AND BECAUSE SHE WAS SO DETERMINED, HE GRANTED HER DESIRE! HER DAUGHTER WAS HEALED FROM THAT VERY MOMENT.

HOW OFTEN DO WE GIVE UP AFTER WE PRAY FOR JUST A WHILE ABOUT SOMETHING SPECIFIC AND SEE NO ANSWERS? WE FEEL AS

IF OUR PRAYERS ARE FALLING ON DEAF EARS. WE MAY EVEN RECEIVE DISCOURAGEMENT FROM OUR FRIENDS AND LOVED ONES FOR PRAYING SO LONG ABOUT SOMETHING SPECIFIC. WE MIGHT FEEL NEGLECTED BY OUR SAVIOR, EVEN AS THIS LADY DID. WE NEED NEVER TO GIVE UP. SOMETIMES OUR FAITH AND DETERMINATION ARE JUST BEING TESTED, ESPECIALLY IF OUR PRAYERS ARE REQUESTS OF SPIRITUAL AND ETERNAL VALUE. THE LORD'S EARS ARE NOT DEAF TO THE CRIES OF HIS CHILDREN.

"KEEP ON ASKING, AND YOU WILL RECEIVE WHAT YOU ASK FOR. KEEP ON SEEKING, AND YOU WILL FIND. KEEP ON KNOCKING, AND THE DOOR WILL BE OPENED TO YOU. FOR EVERYONE WHO ASKS, RECEIVES. EVERYONE WHO SEEKS, FINDS. AND TO EVERYONE WHO KNOCKS, THE DOOR WILL BE OPENED." MATTHEW 7:7-8 (NEW LIVING TRANSLATION)

FROM DARKNESS TO LIGHT!

ONE CLOUDY DAY, WITH CLEANING SPRAY AND TOWEL IN HAND, I STOOD BACK AND ADMIRED MY CRYSTAL CLEAN WINDOWS. HOWEVER, THE FOLLOWING DAY THE SUN SHONE BRIGHTLY AND I WAS ASTONISHED AT THE SIGHT I SAW. TO MY UTTER DISMAY, WHAT HAD LOOKED PERFECTLY CLEAN THE PREVIOUS DAY, THE WINDOWS NOW DISPLAYED A FILM OF SMUT, DIRT, AND SPOTS. MY ATTENTION HAD BEEN BROUGHT TO THE FACT THAT THE BRILLIANCE OF THE SUN SHINING INTO VIEW HAD PUT "A DIFFERENT LIGHT ON THE SUBJECT." I IMMEDIATELY THOUGHT OF HOW AT ONE TIME IN MY LIFE, WITH A SELF RIGHTEOUS ATTITUDE, I HAD ASSUMED THAT I HAD A "SPIC AND SPAN" HEART. THEN ONE DAY JESUS, THE

SON OF GOD, SHINED HIS SPOTLIGHT IN AND EXPOSED SO MUCH TRASH I DID NOT REALIZE EVEN EXISTED. I INVITED HIM TO NOT ONLY EXPOSE, BUT TO ALSO DISPOSE OF MY MUCH HATED SIN. HOW DECEIVED MY HEART HAD BEEN!

OUT CAME THE CLEANING SUPPLIES AGAIN. ALTHOUGH THE WINDOWS HAD TO BE RECLEANED A SECOND TIME, I CAME TO THE CONCLUSION THAT CHRIST DOES A THOROUGH JOB OF CLEANING OUR HEARTS THE FIRST TIME AROUND!

"WHEN JESUS SPOKE AGAIN TO THE PEOPLE, HE SAID, "I AM THE LIGHT OF THE WORLD. WHOEVER FOLLOWS ME WILL NEVER WALK IN DARKNESS, BUT WILL HAVE THE LIGHT OF LIFE." JOHN 8:12 (NEW INTERNATIONAL VERSION)

"THE HEART IS MORE DECEITFUL THAN ALL ELSE AND IS DESPERATELY SICK; WHO CAN UNDERSTAND IT?" JEREMIAH 17:9

AN ELECTRIFYING LESSON FROM THE ELECTRIC HEATER

ONE COLD, DAMP, WINTRY DAY, I COULD NOT SEEM TO GET MYSELF WARM. ALTHOUGH OUR THERMOSTAT WAS TURNED UP, MERELY GLANCING THROUGH THE WINDOW AT THE COLD RAIN OUTSIDE MADE ME SHIVER. OUR LITTLE SPACE HEATER WAS SITUATED ON THE SIDELINES OF OUR DEN AND IT OCCURRED TO ME THAT IF I MOVED CLOSER TO THAT HEATER, I JUST MIGHT ENJOY SOME WARMTH FROM IT. I QUICKLY GRABBED A BOOK, SCOOTED A CHAIR UP CLOSE TO ITS PERMEATING HEAT AND SOON I WAS AS "SNUG AS A BUG IN A RUG" AS THE CLECHE' GOES. I WAS COMFORTABLY SURROUNDED BY ITS HEAT.

SOON AFTER I WAS REFLECTING ON THE FACT OF HOW WARM I HAD BECOME SINCE RELOCATING CLOSER TO THE SOURCE OF HEAT. A SPIRITUAL NUGGET BEGAN TO SURFACE. HOW OFTEN WE BECOME COLD AND INDIFFERENT TOWARD GOD OUR CREATOR. THE HURTS IN LIFE, PERHAPS UNANSWERED PRAYERS, AND WOUNDS INFLICTED BY OUR FELLOWMAN AND EVEN OUR CHRISTIAN BRETHERN SOMETIME DRIVE US AWAY AND WE BECOME DISTANT AND COMPLACENT. INSTEAD OF RUNNING TO OUR SHELTER IN THE TIME OF STORM, WE TEND TO HIBERNATE BY WITHDRAWING AND HANGING WALLS AROUND OUR HEARTS. ALL WE NEED TO DO TO OBTAIN WARMTH AND GRACE, IS TO DRAW CLOSER TO THE LORD, OUR SOURCE. WE CAN DO THIS BY GETTING INTO HIS WORD, RECEIVING STRENGTH FROM OTHER BELIEVERS AND SEEKING HIM DILIGENTLY THROUGH PRAYER. REST ASSURED THAT IN DOING SO, HE WILL DRAW NIGH TO US.

"DRAW NEAR TO GOD AND HE WILL DRAW NEAR TO YOU." JAMES 4:8 (NEW AMERICAN STANDARD)

COVERED BY PRAYER

WHILE FLIPPING THROUGH MY BIBLE ONE DAY, I CAME ACROSS THE PICTURE OF A LITTLE GIRL WE HAD ADOPTED FROM UGANDA. I HAD LONG FORGOTTEN THIS CHILD ALTHOUGH WE HAD MADE A PLEDGE A YEAR OR TWO EARLIER TO SUPPORT HER FINANCIALLY AND WITH PRAYER. THE FINANCIAL SEGMENT HAD LONG BEEN PAID IN FULL, BUT THE PRAYERS HAD SUBSIDED OVER A PERIOD OF TIME. I FELT SO DISAPPOINTED WITH MYSELF WHEN I CAME TO THIS REALIZATION.

MY MIND THEN BEGAN TO FLOW WITH MENTAL PICTURES OF OTHERS I HAD ASSURED OF MY PRAYERS IN THE PAST; YET ONE BY ONE, HAD FORGOTTEN OVER THE PERIOD OF TIME TO LIFT THEIR NEEDS TO

THE THRONE ROOM. HOW REMORSEFUL I WAS. I HAD GOOD INTENTIONS, BUT HAD FAILED.

IT CAME TO MIND HOW THAT ALTHOUGH I HAD UNINTENTIONALLY FORGOTTEN TO PRAY FOR OTHERS SPECIFIC NEEDS I AM NEVER FORGOTTEN! THE HEAVENS ARE BOMBARDED WITH PRAYER ON MY BEHALF BY THE FAITHFULNESS OF THE HOLY SPIRIT AND ALSO OUR LORD.

I CAME TO THE CONCLUSION AND NEW DETERMINATION TO BEGIN PRAYING "ON THE SPOT" WHENEVER POSSIBLE WITH SOMEONE REQUESTING PRAYER. I HAVE FOUND SINCE BEGINNING THIS PRACTICE, THAT MANY TIMES, MY FOCUS IS REINFORCED TO PRAY PRIVATELY LATER FOR THAT SAME NEED AGAIN.

"AND IN THE SAME WAY THE SPIRIT ALSO HELPS OUR WEAKNESS; FOR WE DO NOT KNOW HOW TO PRAY AS WE SHOULD, BUT THE SPIRIT HIMSELF INTERCEDES FOR US WITH GROANINGS TOO DEEP FOR WORDS;

AND HE WHO SEARCHES THE HEARTS KNOWS WHAT THE MIND OF THE SPIRIT IS, BECAUSE HE INTERCEDES FOR THE SAINTS ACCORDING TO THE WILL OF GOD." ROMANS 8:26-27.

"CHRIST JESUS IS HE WHO DIED, YES, RATHER WHO WAS RAISED, WHO IS AT THE RIGHT HAND OF GOD, WHO ALSO INTERCEDES FOR US." ROMANS 8:34 (NEW AMERICAN STANDARD BIBLE)

THOROUGH CLEANSING!

ONE DAY WHILE SHOWERING, I WAS ESPECIALLY DISTRESSED OVER A REOCCURRING SIN. I WAS FEELING AS IF THE TRANSGRESSION WAS JUST TOO GREAT TO BE FORGIVEN. ALTHOUGH I HAD CONFESSED THE SIN TO MY SAVIOR AND ASKED FOR HIS FORGIVENESS, I DID NOT "FEEL" FORGIVEN. I FELT I HAD GONE BEYOND THE POINT OF FORGIVENESS SINCE I KEPT HAVING PROBLEMS WITH THIS SAME REOCCURRING SIN.

SUDDENLY MY EYE CAUGHT A GLIMPSE OF THE LABEL ON A CAN OF CLEANING AGENT SETTING ON THE SHOWER STALL SHELF. THE LABEL BOLDLY CLAIMED, "TOUGH ENOUGH TO CLEAN ANY STAIN!" WOW! GOD GENTLY REMINDED ME THROUGH THIS CLEANING

AGENT THAT THE BLOOD OF JESUS CHRIST WAS POWERFUL--POWERFUL ENOUGH TO CLEANSE ANY STAIN OF SIN! WHAT A REFRESHING AND CLEANSING SHOWER I EXPERIENCED THAT DAY!

"IF WE CONFESS OUR SINS, HE IS FAITHFUL AND JUST TO FORGIVE US OUR SINS, AND TO CLEANSE US FROM ALL UNRIGHTEOUSNESS." I JOHN 1:9 (KING JAMES BIBLE)

MATHEMATICS LESSON LEARNED!

THE SMALL GROUP BIBLE STUDY MEETINGS HELD IN OUR HOME WERE ENRICHING OUR LIVES WITH BOTH SPIRITUAL GROWTH AND CHRISTIAN FELLOWSHIP. BEFORE WE REALIZED WHAT WAS HAPPENING, OUR GROUP HAD OUTGROWN THE FACILITIES OF OUR HOME; A SURE SIGN THAT TIME HAD COME TO "BIRTH" ANOTHER GROUP TO BE HOSTED AT SOMEONE ELSE'S HOME.

THIS WAS A VERY DIFFICULT TASK FOR US AS WE HAD COME TO LOVE EACH ATTENDEE OF THE SMALL GROUP. I ESPECIALLY HAD AN ARDUOUS TIME, HESITANT ABOUT GIVING ANY OF THEM UP TO ANOTHER GROUP.

IT WAS NOT UNTIL A WHILE LATER AS I WAS PONDERING THE SITUATION THAT THE LORD BROUGHT TO MIND THE SCRIPTURE OF THE LOAVES AND FISHES. I WAS REMINDED THAT THE LOAVES AND FISH WERE NOT MULTIPLIED UNTIL JESUS FIRST BLESSED AND BEGAN DIVIDING. I THEN REALIZED THAT IN ORDER TO MULTIPLY AND GROW, IT WOULD BE NECESSARY TO FIRST BLESS AND THEN DIVIDE.

AS DIFFICULT AS IT WAS, WHAT A BLESSING WE HAVE RECEIVED SINCE THAT TIME TO WITNESS SEVERAL SMALL GROUPS BIRTHED BY SIMPLY RELEASING, BLESSING AND DIVIDING. AFTER ALL, THE SMALL GROUP BELONGS TO HIM!

"AND HE TOOK THE FIVE LOAVES AND THE TWO FISH, AND LOOKING UP TOWARD HEAVEN, HE BLESSED THE FOOD AND BROKE THE LOAVES AND HE KEPT GIVING THEM TO THE DISCIPLES TO SET BEFORE THEM; AND HE DIVIDED UP THE TWO FISH AMONG THEM ALL. AND THEY ALL ATE AND WERE SATISFIED." MARK 6:41-42 (NEW AMERICAN STANDARD BIBLE)

LEARNING FROM WOOLY SHEEP

I WATCHED PATIENTLY AS THE SHEEP TOOK THEIR TIME CROSSING OVER THE DUSTY ROAD. WE WERE NEAR THE JERICHO ROAD AND HAD TREMENDOUSLY ENJOYED OUR LONG AWAITED TRIP TO THE HOLY LAND. MANY THINGS I LEARNED WHILE THERE AND THE BIBLE TRULY WAS BROUGHT TO LIFE. BUT NONE OF MY LESSONS WERE AS VALUABLE AND PERTINENT AS THE ONE I LEARNED FROM THESE WOOLY SHEEP.

ONE BY ONE THEY CROSSED OVER AND CAME TO A COMPLETE STANDSTILL ON THE GRASSY SIDE OF A MEADOW. PATIENTLY THEY AWAITED

THE ARRIVAL OF THEIR SHEPHERDESS WHO QUICKLY CAME TO THE FRONT TO LEAD HER FLOCK. ONCE SHE BEGAN HER TREK UP THE HILLSIDE, THEY FOLLOWED CLOSELY BEHIND.

THE LORD GENTLY SPOKE TO MY HEART THAT I SHOULD BE MORE LIKE THOSE SHEEP; NOT SPEEDING AHEAD AND LOSING SIGHT OF THE SHEPHERD, BUT RATHER SHOULD LEARN TO WAIT PATIENTLY FOR THE LEADERSHIP OF MY GOOD SHEPHERD WHO LEADS ME IN THE PATHS OF RIGHTEOUSNESS. SO MANY TIMES I HAVE GONE THROUGH HARDSHIPS DUE TO MY IMPATIENCE AND FAILURE TO WAIT UPON THE LORD'S TIMING. NEITHER SHOULD WE FOLLOW OUR LEADER AT A DISTANCE. WE NEED TO ALWAYS REMAIN WITHIN HIS VIEW.

IT HAS BEEN SAID THAT SHEEP ARE REALLY DUMB ANIMALS. I SURMISE THAT THEY ARE SMARTER THAN WE THINK. THEY AT LEAST HAVE THE WISDOM OF FOLLOWING IN THE SAFETY OF THEIR SHEPHERD.

"I AM THE GOOD SHEPHERD; I KNOW MY OWN SHEEP AND THEY KNOW ME, JUST AS MY FATHER KNOWS ME AND I KNOW THE FATHER. SO I SACRIFICE MY LIFE FOR THE SHEEP." JOHN 10:14 (NEW LIVING TRANSLATION)

PARABLE OF THE SEAGULL

THE SUDDEN COMMOTION OUTSIDE COMPELLED ME TO STOP IN MY TRACKS. I WAS HURRIEDLY PUTTING THE FINISHING TOUCHES ON MY FACE, BUT HAD AN INCLINATION THAT I NEEDED TO STOP AND WATCH. I WAS ABOUT TO LEARN A GREAT LESSON.

AS I GLANCED OUTSIDE MY UPSTAIRS WINDOW, I SAW A STRANGE SIGHT BELOW. MY NEIGHBOR WAS ATTEMPTING TO CREEP UP SLOWLY AND CAUTIOUSLY ON A LARGE SMOKE-COLORED SEAGULL. JUST WITHIN MY NEIGHBOR'S REACH, THE BIRD AWKWARDLY GLIDED UP TO PERCH ON A HIGH FENCE. WHAT AMUSED ME WAS THE FACT THAT ATTACHED TO THE BIRD'S FEET

WAS A LARGE PLASTIC GROCERY BAG WHICH HAD SOMEHOW BECOME ENTANGLED. AS THE BIRD ATTEMPTED TO SOAR UPWARD, HIS FLIGHT WAS LIMITED AS THE BAG EXPANDED WITH AIR AND WEIGHTED HIM DOWN. HE RESEMBLED A SMALL CRITTER ACCOMMODATING A LARGE UPSIDE-DOWN PARACHUTE.

AFTER AWHILE THE SEAGULL WOULD COME DOWN AND AGAIN THE NEIGHBOR WOULD MAKE HIS ATTEMPT TO FREE THE BIRD FROM HIS ENTANGLEMENT, ONLY TO BE LEFT WITH GENTLE WIND FROM THE BIRD'S WINGS FLAPPING IN HIS FACE.

THIS HAPPENED SEVERAL TIMES AND I COULD NOT HELP BUT CHUCKLE AT THIS AMUSING SIGHT UNTIL THE LORD SPOKE SOLEMNLY TO MY HEART. IT WAS A REMINDER OF HOW THE LORD WAS MUCH LIKE MY NEIGHBOR. MY NEIGHBOR WAS THERE TO HELP AND WAS ATTEMPTING TO FREE THE BIRD FROM ITS ENTANGLEMENTS. GOD IS ALWAYS ATTEMPTING TO FREE MANKIND FROM HIS

BURDENS AND IMPRISONMENTS. AS THE BIRD DID NOT TRUST MY NEIGHBOR'S HELP, NEITHER DOES MAN TRUST HIS MAKER, BUT PREFERS TO CARRY HIS BURDENS HIMSELF.

AS THE BIRD COULD NOT SOAR VERY HIGH FOR THE WEIGHT OF THE BAGGAGE, NEITHER CAN MANKIND REACH THE HEAVENLIES WITH THE BURDENS AND BAGGAGE ATTACHED TO HIM… THE BAGGAGE OF FEAR, PRIDE, WORRY, BITTERNESS AND UNBELIEF. GOD REMINDED ME HOW HE WANTS TO FREE US FROM ALL THAT WOULD HOLD US TO THIS OLD WORLD, SO THAT WE MIGHT SOAR HIGH WITH HIM.

WHAT A SOBERING LESSON FROM A SIMPLE OL' SEAGULL.

"THEREFORE, SINCE WE HAVE SO GREAT A CLOUD OF WITNESSES SURROUNDING US, LET US ALSO LAY ASIDE EVERY ENCUMBRANCE, AND THE SIN WHICH SO EASILY ENTANGLES US, AND LET US RUN WITH ENDURANCE THE RACE THAT IS SET BEFORE US, FIXING OUR EYES ON JESUS, THE AUTHOR AND PERFECTER

OF FAITH, WHO FOR THE JOY SET BEFORE
HIM ENDURED THE CROSS, DESPISING THE
SHAME, AND HAS SAT DOWN AT THE RIGHT
HAND OF THE THRONE OF GOD." HEBREWS
12:1-2 (NEW AMERICAN STANDARD BIBLE)

FORGIVING WHEN IT HURTS

WHAT A WEEKEND I'D HAD! I ACTUALLY DREADED SHOWING UP AT WORK AFTER SUCH A MISERABLE WEEKEND. FRIDAY BEFORE I LEFT MY OFFICE, I WAS VERBALLY ATTACKED BY A CO-WORKER. SHE HAD SAID SO MANY UNKIND THINGS AND MADE UNTRUE ACCUSATIONS AGAINST ME. OUR INDIFFERENCES HAD NOT BEEN SETTLED BEFORE I LEFT THAT FRIDAY AFTERNOON AND THE ENTIRE EPISODE HAUNTED ME ALL WEEKEND. IN FACT, THE STORM IN MY MIND HAD ERUPTED INTO A MONSOON ALMOST RESULTING IN CATASTROPHIC DISASTER. THE "TAPE PLAYER" IN MY MIND REPLAYED THE SAME SCENERIO OVER AND OVER WITH EACH OCCURRENCE BECOMING MORE PIERCING! THROUGHOUT THE WEEKEND, I

CRIED OUT TO THE LORD TO ENABLE ME TO FORGIVE HER.

MONDAY MORNING ARRIVED MUCH TOO QUICKLY WITH MY DREADED ENCOUNTER BEING TOP PRIORITY. I ALMOST "BUMPED" INTO HER AS SOON AS I ENTERED THE BUILDING. I WAS SURPRIZED WHEN I HEARD A CHEERY "HELLO" FROM HER AS IF NOTHING HAD EVER HAPPENED ON FRIDAY! WHEN SHE ASKED HOW MY WEEKEND HAD BEEN, A FLOODGATE EXPRESSING WOUNDED MISERY EXPLODED FROM MY HEART. WHEN I SHARED THAT I FELT SHE OWED ME AN APOLOGY, SHE SNARLED AN INSINCERE, "I'M SORRY." WHEN I CONVEYED THAT I HAD PRAYED ALL WEEKEND FOR THE ABILITY TO FORGIVE HER FOR HURTING ME SO, SHE QUICKLY RETORTED, "WELL, YOU MUST NOT HAVE FORGIVEN ME OR YOU WOULD NOT HAVE STRUGGLED ALL WEEKEND LONG!"

I LEFT THE ROOM, NOT FEELING MUCH BETTER AFTER THE CONFRONTATION. I WAS SLIGHTLY CONFUSED AND BEGAN TO WONDER IF, IN REALITY, I HAD FORGIVEN

HER ALTHOUGH I HAD DESPARATELY SOUGHT AND REQUESTED THE LORD'S HELP.

SHORTLY THEREAFTER SETTLING INTO MY OFFICE CHAIR TO BEGIN MY WEEK'S WORK, THE LORD GENTLY SPOKE TO MY SPIRIT. HE INFORMED ME THAT THE VERY FIRST TIME I HAD ASKED FOR HIS ASSISTANCE, THE FORGIVENESS HAD TAKEN PLACE IN THE SPIRIT REALM. I JUST HADN'T BEEN ABLE TO SEE IT IN THE PHYSICAL REALM. HE REMINDED ME OF THE EVENT WHEN HE WAS HANGING ON THE CROSS; HOW HE HAD LOOKED AT THE CROWD AND PRAYED, "FATHER FORGIVE THEM FOR THEY KNOW NOT WHAT THEY DO." HE HAD ACTUALLY FORGIVEN THE ONES WHO WERE CRUCIFYING HIM. YET HE REMINDED ME OF THE PAIN HE BORE IN HIS HANDS AND HIS FEET. WHAT I WAS EXPERIENCING WAS THE PAIN WHICH HAD BEEN INFLICTED BY MY CO-WORKER. TRULY THE FORGIVENESS HAD ALREADY TAKEN EFFECT.

I AM SO THANKFUL FOR THE LORD'S FAITHFULNESS TO FORGIVE US AS WELL AS ENABLE US TO FORGIVE THOSE WHO HAVE

WRONGED US. AFTER ALL, LIFE IS FULL OF HURTS AND IN FORGIVENESS, WE CAN BECOME BETTER PEOPLE, RATHER THAN BITTER PEOPLE. IT IS OUR CHOICE TO FORGIVE OTHERS RATHER THAN HARBORING HATRED. HE IS FAITHFUL TO SOFTEN OUR HEARTS AND TO APPLY THE "BALM OF GILEAD" TO OUR HURTS. WE MAY NOT BE ABLE TO FORGET THE INCIDENT IMMEDIATELY, HOWEVER, WITH TIME, HEALING DOES TAKES PLACE.

"MAKE ALLOWANCE FOR EACH OTHER'S FAULTS, AND FORGIVE ANYONE WHO OFFENDS YOU. REMEMBER, THE LORD FORGAVE YOU, SO YOU MUST FORGIVE OTHERS." COLOSSIANS 3:13 (NEW LIVING TRANSLATION BIBLE)

LIFE LESSON NUMBER THIRTEEN

PAINLESS AGING

ENTRANCED BY WHAT APPEARED IN THE MIRROR, I STOOD GLARING IN UTTER AMAZEMENT! WHAT HAD AT ONE TIME BEEN "CHINA-DOLL" PORCELAIN COMPLEXION SEEMED NOW TO HAVE TURNED OVERNIGHT INTO A BARRAGE OF WRINKLES. WAS I REALLY THIS OLD, WHEN I FELT SO YOUTHFUL INSIDE? WHERE HAD TIME GONE? IT SEEMED LIKE ONLY YESTERDAY THAT I WAS A YOUNG BRIDE WALKING DOWN THE AISLE.

NOW, IN A NEW SEASON OF MY LIFE, I WAS FACING A DIFFICULT NEW CHALLENGE— THAT OF BEING PROMOTED AS A COOKING SPECIALIST VIA TELEVISION AND VARIOUS MEANS. I WONDERED IF I WAS REALLY

CAPABLE OF SUCH A TASK IN THIS PHASE OF MY LIFE. AGING DOES HAVE SOME ADVANTAGES SUCH AS SENIOR DISCOUNTS, BUT THE DISADVANTAGES SUCH AS MEMORY LOSS SEEMED TO BE AN OUTNUMBERING FACTOR...ONE I COULD NOT AFFORD TO DISPLAY WHILE BEING TELEVISED LIVE.

REFLECTING BACK OVER MY LIFE, I CAME TO REALIZE THAT GOD HAD INDEED LED ME STEP BY STEP THROUGH THE VARIOUS STAGES SINCE CHILDHOOD. HE SURELY WAS ABLE TO LEAD ME THROUGH THIS ONE, THE "WINTER SEASON" I WAS QUICKLY APPROACHING. HAD HE NOT BEEN FAITHFUL IN USING MOSES, DANIEL, PAUL, SIMEON, AND ANNA, TO NAME A FEW OF THE BIBLE PEOPLE DURING THEIR SENIOR YEARS?

BY THE TIME I HAD FINISHED STUDYING MY FACE, I FELT DETERMINED THAT GOD WOULD TRULY CONTINUE TO BE WITH AND ENABLE ME RIGHT UP TO THE END—WRINKLES, GRAY HAIR AND ALL!

"EVEN TO YOUR OLD AGE AND GRAY HAIRS
I AM HE, I AM HE WHO WILL SUSTAIN YOU.
I HAVE MADE YOU AND I WILL CARRY YOU; I
WILL SUSTAIN YOU AND I WILL RESCUE YOU."
ISAIAH 46:4 (NEW INTERNATIONAL VERSION)

CONQUERING DEATH!

I WAS DEVASTATED! MY FAITH WAS SHATTERED. ALL MY ADULT CHRISTIAN LIFE HAD LEAD ME TO FIRMLY BELIEVE THAT WHATEVER WE ASKED IN FAITH, BELIEVING, GOD WOULD GIVE IT.

I HAD JUST RECEIVED WORD THAT MY GOOD FRIEND WHO SERVED AS A MISSIONARY IN BRAZIL HAD DIED.

"WHY? AND HOW COULD SHE BE DEAD?" I QUERIED. HAD NOT I PRAYED DILIGENTLY FOR HER HEALING? HER DEATH ANGEL HAD ARRIVED JUST IN THE PRIME OF LIFE WHEN SHE WAS GIVING SO MUCH TO GOD'S KINGDOM AND REACHING SO MANY LIVES FOR HIM. HOW COULD THIS HAVE HAPPENED?

SO MANY PRAYERS HAD GONE UP FOR HER, ABROAD IN HER MISSION AREA OF BRAZIL, AS WELL IN THE UNITED STATES WHERE SHE HAD ITINERATED. I KNEW GOD COULD HEAL HER OF THIS DEADLY CANCEROUS DISEASE, YET HE HAD ALLOWED HER TO DIE. IT JUST DID NOT MAKE SENSE. WERE ALL OF MY PRAYERS IN VAIN? QUESTIONS CONTINUED TO FLOOD MY MIND AND DWINDLE MY FAITH.

SEVERAL WEEKS LATER AS I STILL ASKED "WHY", THE ANSWER FINALLY CAME. AS I STUDIED MY BIBLE, THE VERSES IN ISAIAH 57:1-2 SUDDENLY CAME ALIVE. I BEGAN TO REALIZE THAT GOD WAS OMNIPOTENT AND REGARDLESS OF MY DEMANDS IN PRAYER, HE KNEW WHAT WAS AHEAD FOR MY FRIEND AND DECIDED TO PROTECT HER FROM IT. HE REALLY KNEW WHAT WAS BEST FOR HER AND I DETERMINED, IN REALITY, WHAT IS BEST FOR EACH OF US. MY FAITH AND TRUST WAS RESTORED IN A GOD WHO KNOWS HOW TO CARE FOR HIS OWN. I WAS TOLD THAT SHE PASSED WITH A SMILE ON HER FACE AND PRAISES TO GOD ON HER LIPS AS SHE ENTERED INTO THE HEAVENLY REALM.

"GOOD PEOPLE PASS AWAY; THE GODLY OFTEN DIE BEFORE THEIR TIME. BUT NO ONE SEEMS TO CARE OR WONDER WHY. NO ONE SEEMS TO UNDERSTAND THAT GOD IS PROTECTING THEM FROM THE EVIL TO COME. FOR THOSE WHO FOLLOW GODLY PATHS WILL REST IN PEACE WHEN THEY DIE." ISAIAH 57:1-2 (NEW LIVING TRANSLATION)

THE CHRISTMAS COAT MIRACLE

IT WAS BEGINNING TO LOOK A LOT LIKE CHRISTMAS. THE SCENT OF FRESH GREENERY AND THE BAKING OF COOKIES ACCENTUATED THE AIR. I HAD COMPLETED MY DECORATING AND HAD PLANNED THE ANNUAL FAMILY GET-TOGETHER WITH MY SIBLINGS. MOST OF THEM WOULD BE ARRIVING FROM OUT OF STATE IN MID DECEMBER. ALL PLANS SEEMED TO BE SHAPING UP, WITH THE EXCEPTION OF ONE ITEM. MY HUSBAND AND I ALWAYS DELIGHTED IN SHARING A PERTINENT DEVOTIONAL BEFORE OPENING GIFTS. THIS YEAR BOTH OF US HAD BEEN PRAYING FOR GUIDANCE ON SHARING, BUT NEITHER OF US HAD A CLUE FOR AN APPROPRIATE

MEDITATION. AS OUR FAMILY FUNCTION WAS QUICKLY APPROACHING, I WAS BEGINNING TO BECOME MORE APPREHENSIVE OF NOT BEING TOTALLY PREPARED.

THE MONDAY PRIOR TO THE WEEKEND OF OUR FAMILY PARTY, I WAS AT MY PART TIME JOB WORKING AT THE GIFT SHOP. WE WERE NOT PARTICULARLY BUSY WHEN A HANDSOME COUPLE CAME IN. AFTER OFFERING ASSISTANCE TO THEM, I COMMENTED ON HOW NICE THE LADY LOOKED WITH HER MATCHING EARRINGS & SWEATER. I ALSO EXCLAIMED HOW BEAUTIFUL THE FULL-LENGTH MINK COAT WAS & TEASINGLY ASKED IF I COULD TOUCH IT. THE LADY REPLIED THAT ALTHOUGH IT LOOKED REAL, IT WAS NOT; HOWEVER SHE DID HAVE A "REAL MCCOY" AT HOME. WHEN I INQUIRED WHERE HOME WAS, SHE REPLIED "OKLAHOMA CITY." AFTER CHATTING A FEW MOMENTS, THE COUPLE CONTINUED TO BROWSE WHILE I BEGAN ASSISTING OTHER CUSTOMERS WHICH HAD ARRIVED.

WHILE BUSYING MYSELF WITH OTHER SHOPPERS, I LOST SIGHT OF THE FIRST PATRONS. APPROXIMATELY FIVE OR TEN MINUTES HAD PASSED WHEN THE COUPLE RETURNED & THE GENTLEMEN APPROACHED ME WITH THE OPEN COAT IN HAND ASKING ME TO TRY IT ON FOR SIZE. WHEN I TOLD THEM THAT I COULDN'T DO THAT, HE REMARKED, "THIS IS FOR YOU! MERRY CHRISTMAS!" HE THRUST IT AT ME AND THEY BOTH MADE A QUICK "GET-AWAY" FROM THE STORE, EVEN BEFORE I COULD FIND OUT THEIR NAMES OR THANK THEM.

ONCE REALITY OF THE EVENT HIT, I BEGAN TO HAVE SOME SPIRITUAL NUGGETS DROPPED INTO MY HEART. FIRST, I REALIZED THAT THIS WAS A GIFT GIVEN TO ME BY TOTAL STRANGERS. I HAD DONE NOTHING TO DESERVE IT. GOD REMINDED ME THAT HE GIVES THE GREATEST GIFT WHICH COULD NOT BE EARNED, SALVATION, THROUGH JESUS CHRIST HIS SON. AND AS I HAD THE OPPORTUNITY TO RECEIVE OR REFUSE THE GIFT (I DID MAKE AN ATTEMPT TO REFUSE),

WE ARE RESPONSIBLE TO ACCEPT OR DECLINE GOD'S GIFT.

NEXT I LEARNED THAT JUST AS I HAD TO REMOVE MY OLD COAT TO BE REPLACED AND ADORNED WITH MY NEW, GOD'S WORD TELLS US TO TAKE OFF OUR OLD SINFUL NATURE TO BE REPLACED WITH THE NATURE OF CHRIST. (EPH. 4:22-23)

AND LASTLY, I LEARNED THAT JUST AS I AM COMPLETE IN, AND CAN GO OUT WITH CONFIDENCE INTO LIFE'S STORMS WITH CHRIST, I CERTAINLY COULD GO OUT INTO THE WINTER STORM WITH CONFIDENCE, KNOWING THAT MY NEW COAT WOULD KEEP ME WARM AND SAFE!

OF COURSE, I WAS LEFT WITH TEARS FLOWING FROM MY EYES & A BEAUTIFUL COAT IN MY HANDS, JUST IN TIME FOR THE UPCOMING PREDICTED SNOW STORM. I NOW HAD A DEVOTIONAL TO SHARE WITH MY SIBLINGS AT THE FAMILY PARTY! I ALSO SHARED WITH MANY OTHERS, ESPECIALLY WHEN I WAS COMPLIMENTED ON MY BEAUTIFUL

MINK-LOOING COAT. I INDEED HAD A MERRY CHRISTMAS THAT YEAR, ONE I'LL LONG REMEMBER!

"SINCE YOU HAVE HEARD ABOUT JESUS AND HAVE LEARNED THE TRUTH THAT COMES FROM HIM, THROW OFF YOUR OLD SINFUL NATURE AND YOUR FORMER WAY OF LIFE, WHICH IS CORRUPTED BY LUST AND DECEPTION. INSTEAD, LET THE SPIRIT RENEW YOUR THOUGHTS AND ATTITUDES. PUT ON YOUR NEW NATURE, CREATED TO BE LIKE GOD--TRULY RIGHTEOUS AND HOLY." EPHESIANS 4:21-24 (NEW LIVING TRANSLATION)

LORD, SURELY I'M COMING HOME TO YOU!

THE YEAR WAS 2004. I HAD BEEN HAVING SOME COMPLICATIONS WITH MY HEART-- ATRIAL FIBULATION. MY HUSBAND DECIDED, AFTER MY HAVING SEVERAL UNSUCCESSFUL PROCEDURES PERFORMED, IT WAS TIME FOR SOME SERIOUS ACTION TO BE TAKEN AT DUKE HOSPITAL IN DURHAM, NORTH CAROLINA. MY SURGICAL PROCEDURE WAS SCHEDULED FOR EARLY MORNING WHICH WOULD MEAN A PREVIOUS NIGHT'S STAY AT A NEARBY MOTEL.

THE DAY QUICKLY ARRIVED. THAT MORNING AT HOME, WE ENGAGED IN OUR DAILY READING FROM OUR DEVOTIONAL BOOK. STRANGELY ENOUGH, THE MEDITATION WAS

IN REFERENCE TO A GENTLEMAN WHO HAD LOST HIS WIFE OF MANY YEARS, TO DEATH AND HIS STORY OF HOW GOD HAD ENABLED HIM THROUGHOUT HIS DIFFICULT TIME. THAT NIGHT IN THE MOTEL ROOM BEFORE RETIRING, WE PRAYED TOGETHER AND READ FROM GOD'S WORD. I COULD HARDLY BELIEVE MY EARS WHEN THE WORDS FROM THE BIBLE SELECTION SPOKE ABOUT DEATH AND OF HOW IT IS OUR FINAL ENEMY TO BE CONQUERED. (1 CORINTHIANS 15:26) A RESTLESS NIGHT WAS SPENT WITH ANXIOUS THOUGHTS OF MY UPCOMING EARLY MORNING PROCEDURE.

AS WE CHECKED OUT OF THE MOTEL, I INQUIRED ABOUT KEEPING THE "GUIDEPOSTS MAGAZINE" WHICH HAD BEEN PLACED IN OUR ROOM. THE DESK CLERK ENCOURAGED ME TO TAKE IT WITH ME TO THE HOSPITAL. SHE SAID THAT THEY HAD BEEN PLACED IN EACH ROOM FOR THAT SPECIFIC REASON-- FOR THE PATRONS TO ENJOY.

UPON ARRIVAL AT THE HOSPITAL, THERE WAS MUCH PAPERWORK TO BE FILLED OUT,

AND I WAS THANKFUL FOR THE GOOD
READING I COULD ENJOY WHILE WAITING
TO BE CALLED. I COMPLETED MY PAPERWORK,
SETTLED INTO A CHAIR AND FLIPPANTLY
TURNED TO A SHORT TESTIMONIAL WHICH
LOOKED OF INTEREST. I ABOUT "FLIPPED
OUT" AS I READ THE ARTICLE WRITTEN BY A
YOUNG MOTHER, EXPECTING HER SECOND
CHILD. SHE HAD LOST HER OWN MOTHER
TO DEATH AND THE GRIEVING PROCESS SHE
HAD ENCOUNTERED WAS TREMENDOUS. IT
WAS A FACT THAT MY OWN DAUGHTER WAS
EXPECTING HER SECOND CHILD IN JUST A FEW
MONTHS. MY CIRCUMSTANCES CERTAINLY
COULD IDENTIFY WITH THAT ARTICLE.

I WAS BEGINNING TO PONDER IF THIS WAS A
SIGN FROM GOD GETTING ME PREPARED FOR
LEAVING THIS OLD WORLD. AFTER ALL, THIS
WAS THE THIRD ARTICLE REGARDING DEATH
ENCOUNTERED WITHIN A TWENTY FOUR
HOUR PERIOD. BEFORE I COULD GET TOO IN
DEPTH WITH MY PONDERING, MY THOUGHTS
WERE ABRUPTLY INTERRUPTED BY THE
LOUD SPEAKER CALLING MY NAME. I WAS TO
FOLLOW THE NURSE INTO ROOM NUMBER

SEVEN TO BE PREPARED FOR SURGERY. I WAS THINKING, "ISN'T NUMBER SEVEN GOD'S PERFECT NUMBER FOR COMPLETION?" I HAD DECIDED THAT THIS WAS A SURE SIGN THAT I WOULD NOT MAKE IT ALIVE FROM THAT HOSPITAL!

I HAD ALWAYS HELD A SECRET DREAD OF DEATH. I SUPPOSE TO AN EXTENT, WE ALL FEAR THE UNKNOWN. HOWEVER, I WAS TOTALLY SURPRISED AT MY REACTIONS. I WAS NOT THE LEAST BIT AFRAID. I WAS SO THANKFUL TO HAVE THE PEACE THAT PASSETH ALL UNDERSTANDING!

I AM SO GLAD THAT I EXPERIENCED THAT CONFRONTATION WITH FACING DEATH.

I HAVE COME TO THE CONCLUSION THAT DEATH IS NOT TO BE FEARED BY US AS CHRISTIANS. JESUS WILL BE THERE ON THE OTHER SIDE OF THE JORDAN TO WELCOME US INTO HIS PRESENCE!

"THEN, WHEN OUR DYING BODIES HAVE BEEN TRANSFORMED INTO BODIES THAT

WILL NEVER DIE, THIS SCRIPTURE WILL BE FULFILLED: "DEATH IS SWALLOWED UP IN VICTORY. O DEATH, WHERE IS YOUR VICTORY? O DEATH, WHERE IS YOUR STING?" 1 CORINTHIANS 15:54-44 (NEW LIVING TRANSLATION)

III
POETRY & OUTSTANDING
SPIRITUAL TIDBITS

BABY'S BLESSING

LITTLE HANDS THAT REACH OUT
EYES SO FILLED WITH LOVE
TINY LIPS SO PINK IN HUE
OUR BABY-A GIFT FROM ABOVE.

LORD, PLEASE SEND YOUR ANGELS
TO KEEP AND PROTECT OUR CHILD
LITTLE FEET CAN TEND TO WANDER
GUIDE WITH YOUR HANDS SO MILD.

WE KNOW YOU SENT THIS BLESSING
TO MAKE OUR HOME COMPLETE
HELP US AS PARENTS TO TEACH
    WHAT'S RIGHT
YOUR STANDARDS THUS TO MEET.

LORD TO US THIS CHILD WAS GIVEN
ON LOAN A MERE FEW YEARS
THUS WE GIVE BABE BACK TO YOU
BRUSH AWAY LIFE'S HURTS AND TEARS.

THIS TINY ONE WILL SOON
   BE GROWN
TIME QUICKLY SLIPS AWAY
HELP THIS CHILD TO NE'ER DEPART
OR FROM YOUR PRESENCE STRAY.

PSALMS 127:3

OUR DAUGHTER PRESENTED US WITH A LARGE GIFT BOX THE CHRISTMAS OF 2001. ENCLOSED WAS A CARD CONGRATULATING US WITH THE NEWS OF EXPECTING OUR FIRST GRANDCHILD! WHAT A SURPRISE! ALONG WITH THE CARD WAS A REQUEST TO WRITE AND DEDICATE A POEM TO THE NEW GRANDBABY. IT WAS NOT UNTIL SPRING THAT I COULD EVEN FOCUS ON THE FACT THAT I WOULD FINALLY BE HOLDING A BABY IN MY ARMS THE UPCOMING FALL. THE WRITING OF THE POEM WAS LABORIOUS, ESPECIALLY SINCE IT REQUIRED BEING WRITTEN IN UNISEX STYLE, WITHOUT THE KNOWLEDGE OF HAVING A BABY BOY OR GIRL. THE POEM FINALLY ARRIVED IN LATE SPRING. OUR LITTLE BUNDLE OF JOY, PRECIOUS GRANDDAUGHTER ARRIVED IN AUGUST, 2002.

HOUSE BLESSING

MAY THIS HOUSE BE BLESSED OF YOU
AND COVERED BY YOUR CARE.
MAY IT BE A HAVEN
AND A REFUGE OF DAILY PRAYER.
MAY ALL WHO ENTER SENSE YOUR PEACE
AND BLESSINGS FROM ABOVE.
MAY EVERY WORD BE SPOKEN
IN SINCERITY AND LOVE.
MAY YOU BE AT EVERY MEAL
OUR SECRET FRIEND AND GUEST.
AND MAY YOU BRING THE VICTORY
THROUGH EVERY TRIAL AND TEST.
OUR HOME IS GIVEN TO YOU THIS DAY
WE ASK YOU TO ABIDE.
MAY WE LIVE IN PEACE AS A FAMILY
AS YOU RICHLY DWELL INSIDE.

DEUTERNOMY 20:4-5

MY NEICE AND HER HUSBAND HAD JUST BUILT A NEW HOME IN KNOXVILLE, TENNESSEE. SHE REQUESTED THAT MY HUSBAND AND I DEDICATE IT TO THE LORD FOR THEM WHEN WE VISITED FROM VIRGINIA. TIME PASSED WITH THE VISIT BEING CUT SHORT AND THE HOUSE DEDICATION DID NOT COME TO FRUITION.

AT HOME, BACK IN VIRGINIA, REALIZING MY NEICE PROBABLY WAS VERY DISAPPOINTED, I SAT DOWN TO WRITE HER A NOTE OF APOLOGY. NEXT THING I KNEW, THIS POEM WAS THE PRODUCT PENNED AT THE END OF THE LETTER. I WAS GOING TO FOLD UP THE SHEET OF PAPER AND DROP IT IN AN ENVELOPE TO BE MAILED. AFTER READING IT TO MY DAUGHTER, SHE PROMPTED ME TO HAVE IT COPYWRITTEN, SCRIPTED IN CALLIGRAPHY, MATTED AND FRAMED BEFORE MAILING IT TO MY NEICE.

MANY OTHERS DESIRED TO PURCHASE A COPY OF THE FRAMED WORK, WHICH RESULTED IN MY ESTABLISHING A SMALL HOME-BASED BUSINESS NAMED "BECKY'S BLESSINGS." THE

INITIAL SELLS OF THE FINISHED PRODUCT ACTUALLY ASSISTED IN PAYING MY ENTIRE EXPENSE FOR A MISSION TRIP TO COSTA RICA. WHAT A BLESSING THE "HOUSE BLESSING" WAS TO ME.

THE SECRET PLACE

OF TIMES I FEEL SO AFRAID AND ALONE
OH WHERE CAN I GO TO HIDE?
NO ONE SEEMS TO UNDERSTAND
THERE'S NO ONE TO BE BY MY SIDE.

ALAS! I KNOW EXACTLY WHERE TO GO!
I'LL ESCAPE TO THE FRIEND IN MY HEART
HE ABIDES WITHIN THE SECRET PLACE
HE IS THERE AND HE'LL NEVER DEPART.

THIS FRIEND IS THERE ALWAYS
WAITING FOR ME
HE'LL UNDERSTAND, FOR
HE'S BEEN THERE, TOO.
BEFORE I CAN TELL HIM THE
TROUBLES I HAVE
IT SEEMS THAT HE ALREADY KNEW.

I AM SO GLAD THAT I HAVE THIS FRIEND
AND THE SECRET PLACE IN MY HEART

IT SEEMS SO GOOD TO GET AWAY
AND TO OBTAIN A BRAND NEW START.

OH SELF, DON'T WORRY OR DESPAIR
OR ALLOW YOUR HEART TO BE BLUE
JUST RUSH TO HIM, YOUR ENDLESS FRIEND
HE'S THERE JUST WAITING FOR YOU!

THIS POEM WAS PENNED IN 1977 AS I WAS EXPERIENCING A DARK SEASON IN MY LIFE. IT HAS SINCE BEEN COPYWRITTEN AND CONVERTED TO A CARD OF ENCOURAGEMENT. I INVITE YOU TO BE ENCOURAGED BY THE MESSAGE OF THIS POEM.

OUTSTANDING SPIRITUAL TIDBITS

THROUGHOUT MY CHRISTIAN JOURNEY THERE HAVE BEEN SEVERAL OUTSTANDING SPIRITUAL NOUGATS WHICH HAVE ENRICHED MY LIFE. I WILL SHARE THESE WITH YOU IN HOPES THAT YOU WILL BE INSPIRED AS WELL.

IN A BOOK WRITTEN BY CORRIE TEN BOON, SHE ENCOURAGED THE READER TO ENVISION THINGS AS GOD SEES THEM. SHE STATED THAT WE FREQUENTLY SEE THE UNDERSIDE OF A TAPESTRY OF OUR LIFE--THE UGLINESS, THE LOOSE THREADS, AND SOMETIMES THE TANGLEMENTS. GOD SEES THE TOP SIDE, THE FINISHED PRODUCT, THE BEAUTIFUL MASTERPIECE!

I ONCE HEARD THE STORY OF A MAN WHO ATTENDED A REVIVAL AND AFTER EACH NIGHT'S SERVICE, HE WOULD KNEEL AT THE ALTAR AND CRY OUT TO GOD, "LORD, PLEASE REMOVE THESE COBWEBS IN MY HEART." AFTER SEVERAL NIGHTS OF THE SAME PROCEDURE, THE VISITING EVANGELIST CAME UP FROM BEHIND THE MAN KNEELING AND ASSERTED, "LORD, JUST KILL THAT SPIDER!"

SEVERAL YEARS AGO, A RADIO PREACHER RELATED THE EPISODE OF A GENTLEMAN IN THE LATE 1800'S WHO HAD PURCHASED A TICKET TO BOARD A SHIP ACROSS THE OCEAN. HE PACKED ENOUGH CHEESE AND CRACKERS TO LAST HIM THE ENTIRE TRIP. UPON THE ARRIVAL TO THEIR DESTINATION, THE CAPTAIN STOOD AT THE EXIT FAREWELLING EACH PASSENGER AS THEY DEPARTED. WHEN THE GENTLEMAN APPROACHED, THE CAPTAIN EXCLAIMED, "I NOTICED THAT YOU NEVER CAME TO OUR DINING AREA TO ENJOY THE FOOD. DID YOU THINK IT WOULD NOT BE TASTY ENOUGH FOR YOU? "THE GENTLEMAN HUMBLY REPLIED, "I ONLY PURCHASED A TICKET FOR THE VOYAGE OVER, NOT FOR THE FOOD." "OH," EXCLAIMED THE CAPTAIN, "THE FOOD WAS INCLUDED WITH THE TICKET'S PRICE!"

HOW OFTEN, WE DO NOT TAKE ADVANTAGE OF THE FULL PRICE OF CALVARY! OUR SAL-VATION, OUR HEALINGS AND ATONEMENT FOR SIN ARE THE FULL PRICE OUR SAVIOR PAID FOR US ON THE CROSS. WE SOMETIMES LIVE AS A PAUPER RATHER THAN A KING'S KID!

IT HAS BEEN SAID THAT LIFE IS A JOURNEY--FROM BIRTH, A PROCESS LEARNING TO PREPARE FOR DEATH. IN A SENSE IT IS. HOWEVER, LIFE'S JOURNEY CAN TAKE US IN SO MANY DIRECTIONS; SO MANY MOUNTAINS TO CLIMB AND SO MANY VALLEYS TO CROSS OVER.

SOMETIMES SO MUCH FUN AND EXCITEMENT AND OTHER TIMES, SO MUCH DESPAIR AND TRIALS TO OVERCOME.

REGARDLESS, WITH THE CROSS OF JESUS CHRIST AND THE EMPTY TOMB AS OUR FOCAL POINT, LIFE CAN BE MADE BEARABLE AND WE CAN EVEN EXPERIENCE ABUNDANT LIFE. WE ARE INDEED MORE THAN CONQUERERS THROUGH CHRIST WHO STRENGTHENS US.

PACKED WITH EPISODES OF UP AND DOWN EVERYDAY LIVING, THIS BOOK HOPEFULLY WILL INSPIRE THE READER AND ENCOURAGE TO "PRESS ONWARD" TO BECOME AN OVERCOMER AND EXPERIENCE VICTORIOUS LIVING.

REBECCA SEATON, APPROACHING MARRIAGE THE HALF CENTURY MARK, RESIDES WITH HER HUSBAND IN SEVIERVILLE, TENNESSEE. SEVIERVILLE IS HIS HOMETOWN. SINCE HE WENT TO SCHOOL WITH DOLLY PARTON, REBECCA JOKES THAT HE MARRIED HER INSTEAD OF DOLLY BECAUSE SHE COULD COOK AND DOLLY COULD ONLY SING. REBECCA, BEING THE MOTHER OF TWO, ENJOYS HER THREE GRANDKIDS SINCE THEY HAVE RELOCATED TO THE SAME AREA.

AS A FREE-LANCE WRITER, MANY OF HER WRITINGS HAVE BEEN PUBLISHED IN CHRISTIAN MAGAZINES AND DEVOTIONAL BOOKS. SHE HAS ALSO PUBLISHED A COOKBOOK ENTITLED "BECKY'S FAVORITES" WHILE BEING EMPLOYED AS CREATIVE FOOD SPECIALIST AT A SMOKY MOUNTAIN TOURIST

FOOD/ GIFT SHOP. MANY OF HER RECIPES
HAVE BEEN PRESENTED TO A TELEVISION
AUDIENCE PERFORMANCE OVER A PERIOD
OF TIME.

HAVING TAUGHT IN A PRIVATE, CHRISTIAN
PRESCHOOL, AND ALSO SERVING
AS CHILDREN'S PASTOR AT A LARGE
CONGREGATIONAL CHURCH IN HAMPTON,
VIRGINIA, CHILDREN HAVE PLAYED AN
INTEGRAL PART OF HER LIFE. HAVING SERVED
AS LEADER OF BIBLE STUDY GROUP HAS
READIED HER TO SHARE THE GOSPEL WITH
THE HURTING AND WITH ANYONE WHO
WILL LEND AN EAR.

HAVING EXPERIENCED THE UPS AND
DOWNS OF LIFE, SHE HAS LEARNED TO
LIVE VICTORIOUSLY THROUGH THE TRIALS.
THE MANY REQUESTS BY FRIENDS AND
ACQUAINTANCES RESULTED IN THE WRITING
OF THIS BOOK. SHE HOPES ALL WHO READ IT
WILL BE INSPIRED.